THE PLAIN PEOPLE OF BOSTON, 1830–1860

THE URBAN LIFE IN AMERICA SERIES

RICHARD C. WADE, GENERAL EDITOR

STANLEY BUDER
PULLMAN: An Experiment in Industrial Order and Community Planning, 1880–1930

ALLEN F. DAVIS
SPEARHEADS FOR REFORM: The Social Settlements and the Progressive Movement, 1890–1914

LYLE W. DORSETT
THE PENDERGAST MACHINE

JOSEPH M. HAWES
CHILDREN IN URBAN SOCIETY: Juvenile Delinquency in Nineteenth-Century America

MELVIN G. HOLLI
REFORM IN DETROIT: Hazen S. Pingree and Urban Politics

KENNETH T. JACKSON
THE KU KLUX KLAN IN THE CITY, 1915–1930

PETER R. KNIGHTS
THE PLAIN PEOPLE OF BOSTON, 1830–1860: A Study in City Growth

ZANE L. MILLER
BOSS COX'S CINCINNATI: Urban Politics in the Progressive Era

RAYMOND A. MOHL
POVERTY IN NEW YORK, 1783–1825

HUMBERT S. NELLI
ITALIANS IN CHICAGO, 1890–1930: A Study in Ethnic Mobility

JAMES F. RICHARDSON
THE NEW YORK POLICE: Colonial Times to 1901

PETER J. SCHMITT
BACK TO NATURE: The Arcadian Myth in Urban America, 1900–1930

THE PLAIN PEOPLE OF BOSTON, 1830–1860:

A Study in City Growth

PETER R. KNIGHTS

NEW YORK
OXFORD UNIVERSITY PRESS
1971

For my Mother

Library of Congress Catalogue Card Number: 74–159647
Printed in the United States of America

Foreword

Sometimes the most elementary and important historical facts are extraordinarily elusive. In reconstructing the urban experience of the American people, for example, scholars are never quite sure how many people lived in a city at a particular time, how long they had been there, where they came from, or how long they stayed. It is no problem to identify the prominent, the rich and successful, or even the notorious. Yet the ordinary are easily lost in the fragmentary documentation that survives the attrition of time.

In this volume Peter Knights ingeniously recovers this lost dimension of a part of Boston's past. By using modern statistical methods, he re-creates the comings and goings of a significant urban population. Rather than the still-life portrait of conventional reconstructions, he presents almost a moving picture. To be sure, there are no faces, no flesh and bones, but there are the quite human traces of birth and death, residential change, the rise and fall of status, and the movement of people. He has, in short, been able to speak of a whole population statistically without dehumanizing it.

The choice of Boston between 1830 and 1860 is a happy one. For we already know a good deal about its first families, its intelligentsia, and its cultural life from the work of other scholars. Mr. Knights provides us with its indispensable people, those who conducted its everyday affairs, or—in his categories—those engaged in unskilled work and menial service, the semi-skilled and service personnel, petty proprietors, managers and officials, skilled labor, clerical and sales help, semi-professionals, proprietors, managers and professional people. We even learn something about the "miscellaneous and unknown."

This volume will give no reassurance to those who think that American mobility is the product of twentieth-century technology or the automobile, or even affluence. For the author finds a city in constant movement without any trace of these elements. Nearly everyone is on the go; some stayed in the Hub so briefly that they eluded the head counters. Some remain over many years, of course, but their stability is unusual and is often accompanied by constant residential shifts. This kinetic quality of urban life is one of the main themes of Mr. Knights's book.

There is even less reassurance in this volume for those who think that nineteenth-century cities were centers of great upward mobility. The author is charmingly modest in making generalizations about this persistent historical problem, but the scholarly comfort will rest with those who see less "rags to riches" than a lot. Though for many immigrants from Ireland's reluctant and blighted soil the move from wretchedness to rags might have provided some improvement, in Boston the road up was long and difficult. And those who rose usually did so after being born with a head start.

Moreover, in choosing the three decades before the Civil War, the author has provided an additional service. For this period has been badly neglected by even urban historians. Yet it was a time of extraordinary urban growth; the city took off, so to speak, in these years. Though Boston was not the first of the exploding cities, it did undergo very substantial expansion. Hence its experience was far from parochial, providing us with a framework if not a model for analyzing other large cities in the same period. In fine, this is urban not local history.

Some readers when fingering through this book may flinch on seeing its many tables and extensive statistical scaffolding—an understandable reaction, but unwarranted. Mr. Knights carries the quantitative apparatus easily and leads even those who cannot handle long division through the figures and calculus with a helping hand. In addition, his general learning and good sense give the lay reader confidence that no tricks are being played, and his wit and lucidity make it even fun. Moreover, the author, being a good historian, knows he has raised as many questions as he has answered. This is the first sortie of the *Urban Life in America Series* into what is now known as "quantitative history." It won't be the last.

RICHARD C. WADE
GENERAL EDITOR
URBAN LIFE IN AMERICA SERIES

New York, N.Y.
May 1971

Acknowledgments

This is the first of three studies I plan concerning various aspects of the history of Boston, Massachusetts. Since it in a sense serves as a prologue, it is much more concerned with empirical data than the subsequent studies. The second study will examine internal migration to and from Boston, 1850–80, while the third will provide a social analysis of Boston's political leadership from about 1830 on. The latter study will be done in collaboration with Professor Paul Kleppner.

Much of whatever merit this study may possess is due to many individuals who provided released time, money, or information, all three of which the study consumed avidly. Without my employment during 1966–68 as a research assistant in project GS-921, "Ecological Patterns in American Cities: Some Quantitative Studies in Urban History," the basic data would never have been collected. Project GS-921 was funded by the National Science Foundation and by the University of Wisconsin Graduate School. Professor Leo F. Schnore (Sociology) directed the project. I am grateful to him for acquiescing in my desire to collect data on the spot, and for giving me free rein to do so.

During the summer of 1968, the University of Wisconsin provided unanticipated aid in the form of a University Fellowship, while during 1968/69 I benefited from the largesse of the Department of History at the University of Pittsburgh, which awarded me an Andrew Mellon Fellowship. More important, I enjoyed contact with, and gained stimulation from, the members of that department, chaired by Professor Samuel P. Hays. I hope he finds my efforts worthy of his investment. Members of his department, Professors Walter S. Glazer, J. Jonathan Levine (Editor of *Historical Methods Newsletter*), Laurence F. Glasco, and Paul Kleppner (now at Northern Illinois University), provided general and specific criticisms, and acted as sounding boards. Professor Kleppner was kind enough to go over Chapters V, VI, and VII with special care, as well as to read page proof of this book.

As publication drew nigh, Professors Robert W. Fogel (University of Chicago), Richard J. Jensen (University of Illinois at Chicago Circle), John Modell (University of Minnesota), and Frederic C. Jaher (University of Illinois) provided criticism and aid. Naturally, the efforts of those colleagues contributed significantly to the development of this study, but since I did not accept some of their suggestions, they should not be blamed for its shortcomings.

Libraries, surprisingly, contained only a small fraction of the data exploited in this study. I received courteous and uniformly conscientious help from the staffs of the Library of the State Historical Society of Wisconsin and the Memorial Library of the University of Wisconsin, as well as Widener Library at Harvard College, which granted me stack access. At the Boston Athenaeum Reference Department, the late Miss Susan Parsons (in the study's initial phase) and (later) Mr. James E. Belliveau made available Boston City Documents and city directories, together with ancillary materials from the Athenaeum's collections.

The Baker Library of the Harvard Graduate School of Business Administration, through its then head of the Circulation Department, Mr. George Beal, opened its stacks to me, particularly its rich materials on transportation, most of which I did not use, but hope not to waste. In the Manuscripts Division, Mrs. Eleanor C. Bishop and Mr. Robert W. Lovett, Curator, provided, amidst their regular duties, a haven to discuss and theorize about findings.

Public officials opened many doors. At the Massachusetts State House, in the Division of Vital Statistics, Mr. Raymond D. Lavallee, Deputy Secretary of the Commonwealth, then Registrar of the Commonwealth, permitted me to use the state vital statistics records, dating from 1841/42. His successor as Registrar, then Head

Administrative Clerk, Mr. Edward C. Kloza, continued the permission, and in other ways lightened the drudgery of prolonged burrowing in those records.

In the State House basement, at the Massachusetts Archives, Mr. Leo Flaherty, Curator, and Mrs. Flaherty watch over manuscript copies of the federal censuses of Massachusetts for 1850 and 1860; these proved particularly useful in tracing out-migrants from Boston. Mr. Flaherty early called my attention to the Division of Vital Statistics, for which I am especially indebted to him, as it changed the process of finding out-migrants from retail to wholesale.

At the city level, in the City Registrar's Office, William J. Kane, Registrar, arranged access to Boston's birth, death, and marriage records, which were valuable for the years antedating the beginning of the state records. On a day-to-day basis, William F. McOsker, then Deposition Clerk, now Head Clerk, and Charles Jessoe, Senior Clerk (Deaths), aided in guiding me through the thousands of volumes in their care.

Much of the financial information in this study was culled from the records of the city assessors, which seem to be complete from at least the year 1783. Mr. Henry Ireland, now retired, then Head Administrative Clerk, of the Assessing Department, literally provided the key to the vault containing those records. Later visits, in the fall of 1970, were facilitated by Mmes. Margaret Taft and June O'Callaghan of the Assessing Department. These records are kept on dusty shelves in the basement of the Old City Hall Annex, prey to dust, flooding, and janitorial archival care. I hope that Boston's imposing New City Hall will find space to preserve this unique collection. At a critical moment in the harvesting of data from the assessing records, Mr. Edward Fitzpatrick of the Boston Redevelopment Authority provided Xerox facilities, a real boon.

At Boston's Mount Hope Cemetery, Messrs. Philip Fallo, Supervisor of Cemeteries, and Frank Havlin, Clerk, allowed me access to their early interment indices. At private cemeteries, Mount Auburn, the oldest, and Forest Hills both felt their obligations toward their clients precluded outside consultation of interment indices. The most pleasant exception to this was that of Mr. Axel H.

Pamp, Superintendent of Woodlawn Cemetery in Everett, who not only opened to me that cemetery's interment indices, but also lent me several city directories from its collection.

It is distinctly not a pleasure to report that part of the original plan of this study had to be abandoned due to what can be charitably described as an act of gross negligence. In addition to economic data from the Boston assessment records, this study was to have contained extensive information—with anonymity preserved—from individuals' savings accounts. At the Provident Institution for Savings in the Town of Boston, America's oldest operating savings bank, Mr. Hayward S. Houghton, Assistant Vice-President, and Mrs. Bernice D. Parks, Vice-President, permitted me to examine original depositors' records dating to 1816 and account number 1. When I returned to the bank after nineteen months, ready to exploit the records, it was to learn that a bank official had ordered the destruction, without microfilming, of the first century of the bank's precious records. This act, which has foreclosed to us invaluable economic knowledge of the behavior of thousands of ordinary people, is all the more tragic in view of Mr. Houghton's and Mrs. Parks's earlier assurances to me that the bank was well aware of the great historical worth of its records.

At Boston's second oldest savings bank, then the Warren Institution for Savings (1829), now the Union-Warren Savings Bank, Mr. Albert E. Pfefferle, President, explained that the bank had kept inviolate all its old records and intended to continue doing so. But Messrs. S. Lyle Hall of the Boston Five Cents Savings Bank (1854) and Herbert W. Gray of the Suffolk (1833) Franklin Savings Bank were both willing to grant access to their early records. Although this part of the study was frustrated, it is pleasant to report that the Suffolk Franklin later deposited a quantity of its old records with the Baker Library.

Professor Stephan A. Thernstrom (University of California, Los Angeles) graciously allowed me to use a socioeconomic classification scheme he will employ in his forthcoming study, *Migration and Social Mobility in Boston, 1880–1968: A Study in the New Urban History* (Cambridge: Harvard University Press, 1971). The scheme appears in Chapters V and VI; the occupations are listed in Appendix E. Our joint use of this scheme should permit comparisons of our findings on changes in Boston's work force over an extended period.

Among fellow graduate students at the University of Wisconsin, I wish to single out Donald L. Shaw (University of North Carolina), Carl V. Harris (University of California, Santa Barbara), Carl G. Ryant (University of Louisville), and Miss Margaret Walsh (Department of American Studies, University of Keele). They all gave help and encouragement in many dark hours.

The original version of this manuscript was typed by Miss Josephine Stagno of the Department of Sociology, University of Pittsburgh, whom I would like to thank for demonstrating that, for small systems, entropy flow may be reversed.

Too seldom do booksellers receive their due as intermediaries in the world of scholarship. Everyone who has visited George Gloss's Brattle Book Shop in Boston knows that he assuredly deserves recognition for his success in operating "America's Oldest Continuous Antiquarian Book Shop" despite urban renewal projects.

Many others contributed peripherally to this study. I hope that they, and anyone deserving specific mention who was inadvertently omitted, will rest content with a blanket acknowledgment of my gratitude.

In closing, I wish to thank above all Professor Eric E. Lampard (State University of New York, Stony Brook), who as my dissertation adviser at the University of Wisconsin impressed upon me the necessity of putting one's best foot forward from well-constructed scaffolding.

Champaign, Illinois P. R. K.
May 1971

Contents

Tables

Maps

THE PLAIN PEOPLE OF BOSTON, 1830–1860

Men of literary taste or clerical habits are always apt to overlook the working-classes, and to confine the records they make of their own times, in a great degree, to the habits and fortunes of their own associates, or to those of people of superior rank to themselves, of whose sayings and doings their vanity, as well as their curiosity, leads them to most carefully inform themselves. The dumb masses have often been so lost in this shadow of egotism, that, in later days, it has been impossible to discern the very real influence their character and condition has had on the fortune and fate of nations.

FREDERICK LAW OLMSTED, *A Journey in the Seaboard Slave States, with Remarks on Their Economy* (New York: Dix & Edwards, 1856), 214–15.

Introduction

We need fewer studies of the city in history than of the history of cities . . . only the detailed tracing of an immense range of variables, in context, will illuminate the dynamics of the processes here outlined. . . . we shall only learn [about urban developments] when we make out the interplay among them by focusing upon *a* city in all its uniqueness.

OSCAR HANDLIN[1]

The best procedure, therefore, seemed to be one that takes into consideration the finite range of man's life and the finite quality of the reader's patience with and interest in statistics; and this procedure is to use the sampling method.

FRANK L. OWSLEY[2]

The inquirer never starts with a specific question and proceeds to assemble the data, but starts with the whole body of data and asks questions. After all, what is a collection of historical data but a collection of answers waiting to be questioned?

MARSHALL SMELSER and WILLIAM DAVISSON[3]

This study inquires into the history of an important American city by investigating what was happening among that city's people—insofar as social and economic records can tell us—during the years from 1830 to 1860. There are two principal reasons for this study: curiosity, and a desire to devise new historical research methods.

There are many studies of American cities, but very few proceed from the basis of population, for dealing with the characteristics of such elemental constituents of cities is tedious beyond belief, and requires exceptional dedication or resources or—at the very least—considerable initial naïveté. This study aims to provide data which researchers dealing similarly with other cities or with urban theory may alter, amplify, use to build models, or discard, but, it is hoped, not neglect.* Rather than finding hypotheses here, readers will note a *hypotheses non fingo* approach, for at this stage of development of urban researches I concur with Mr. Holmes: "It is a capital mistake, Watson, to theorize without data." But one may ask questions.

To judge how much credence to lend this study's findings, readers are entitled to know, generally, how its results were obtained. The study began with one question: "Given available data, what can one say about the population of ante-bellum (1830–60) Boston?" Ideally, one would start with a complete analysis of Boston's censuses, and move on to supporting materials. Since "Life is short, but the art is long," individual researchers turn perforce to sampling methods.

Between 1830 and 1860, Boston underwent censuses as follows:

Governmental Sponsor	*Years*
Federal	*1830, 1840, 1850, 1860*
State	1840, 1850, *1855*
City	1835, 1845, 1855

For the years *1830, '40, '50, '55,* and *'60* one may obtain microfilms of the original manuscript returns; other years' returns were not located and are presumably lost. In drawing samples, this study used only the federal censuses.

Ante-bellum federal censuses fall into two general categories, mediocre and pathetic. It is unrealistic to demand too much of a data compilation system which operated discontinuously, which was dismantled after use, and which was intended principally to

* An example is David Ward's *Cities and Immigrants* (New York: Oxford University Press, 1971), received while this book was being proofread.

determine the distribution of seats in the House of Representatives. Competent statisticians did not seize control of the census till the late 1840's; thus the censuses of 1830 and 1840 qualify as pathetic, while those of 1850 and 1860 are mediocre. But they are all we have.[4]

The relevant censuses provide us with the principal kinds of information noted in Table Int-1. Other questions, such as physical

Table Int-1. Principal Kinds of Information Provided by the Manuscript Federal Census Returns of 1830/1840/1850/1860

Kind of Information in Census	*Census*			
	1830	*1840*	*1850*	*1860*
Name and sex of household head	yes	yes	yes	yes
Names of household members	no	no	yes	yes
Sex of household members	yes	yes	yes	yes
Age of household members to nearest ____ years	5 or 10	5 or 10	1	1
Number of persons in household	yes	yes	yes	yes
Occupation of adult household members	generic		specific	
Birthplace of household members	no	no	yes	yes
Value of real estate owned by household members	no	no	yes	yes
Value of personal property owned by household members	no	no	no	yes

Source: Manuscript federal census returns, 1830-1860 (on microfilm from National Archives.)

condition (deaf, blind, insane), marital state (married within past year), and educational attainments (in school, literate) need not concern us, for there is abundant internal (as well as contemporary) evidence that these data were poorly gathered—when they were gathered at all.[5]

Since the purpose of this study was to learn about people, and since the only persons listed by name in all four censuses were heads of household, they became the basis of the study. From each of the four censuses, a random sample, of 385 heads of household, stratified* by wards, was drawn, yielding a total of 1540 sample members, who are collectively the subject of this study. Accepting a confidence level of 95 per cent and a confidence interval of plus or minus 5 per cent, a sample of size 385 will be adequate for universes of more than 500,000.[6] (The largest universe actually encountered in the study was of 33,633 households.) One may interpret the above parameters thus: If we were to draw an indefinitely large number of samples of size 385, the results from 95 per cent of these samples would be within 5 per cent of the "true" values for the population from which the samples were drawn, that is, values coming from a complete census of the entire population. Greater sample sizes increase our confidence and narrow the margin of error, as Table Int-2 shows.

Table Int-2. Sample Sizes Required to Sample a Universe of Size 500,000 under Given Conditions

Conditions		*Necessary Sample Size*
Confidence Level	*Confidence Interval*	
95%	± 5%	385 (used in this study)
95%	± 4%	600
99%	± 5%	663
99%	± 4%	1035

Source: Herbert Arkin and Raymond R. Colton, comps., *Tables for Statisticians* (New York: Barnes & Noble, 1963), 145-146 (Table 20).

Researchers with limited time, patience, or resources should make sail conformable with the weather.

There are as yet no published figures on the number of households at the ward level for any ante-bellum federal census, for

* Each ward contributed a part of the sample proportional to that ward's share of Boston's households.

the excellent reason that no one has done the counting. One may circumvent this problem for a whole city by using household running numbers given in the 1850 and 1860 manuscript census schedules to obtain figures for average household size. Applying this figure to pre-1850 city population totals will yield rough-and-ready estimates of the total number of households one must contend with. This permits the researcher to set an upper limit on the size of his universe, and to get some idea of his sample size. Prudent investigators may wish to snatch caution from the winds and use values for universe size 500,000, which should serve for all cities up to at least two million. But there is no evading the necessity, if random sampling and stratification are to be used, of counting and classifying (sex, race) all household heads in all wards of all censuses under examination. Investigators unwilling to invest six months or so in doing this may wish to turn to systematic sampling (taking every *n*th household) methods.

Once one has isolated the sample members, he needs supplemental information on them. This study exploited a variety of such sources, among them city directories, city tax records, the Massachusetts registration system (births, marriages, deaths), the extensive published *Vital Records* volumes, and cemetery interment indices. It was denied access to savings bank records. Table Int-3 indicates the kinds of information one may reasonably anticipate finding in such records.

City directories are probably the most valuable of the supplemental information sources, but they cannot be accepted at face value, and amply repay extended study (see Appendix A, "Using City Directories in Ante-Bellum Urban Historical Research"). Their principal contribution is in helping differentiate sample members from the commonalty by providing address and occupation. Many sample members in this study possessed names such as Bezaleel Bennett or Randall Lufkin, but what of others named Samuel Smith, John O'Brien, or (the ultimate) John Sullivan? These last become more tractable when they are linked to an address; researchers having selected a sample member in a census may look him up in a directory, follow him through the next

Table Int-3. Categories of Information Ordinarily Obtainable about Sample Members from Various Sources

	Sources					
Categories of Information	*City Directories*	*City Tax Records*	*State Registration System*	*Cemetery Interment Indices*	*Savings Bank Records*	Vital Records *Volumes*
Name	x	x	o	o	o	o
Home address	x	x	o	o	o	—
Business address	x	x	—	—	—	—
Occupation	x	x	o	o	o	—
Age	—	—	o	—	o	o
Birthplace	—	—	o	o	—	o
Value of real estate	—	x	—	—	—	—
Value of personal estate	—	x	—	—	—	—
U.S. citizen	—	x	—	—	—	o
Amount of savings	—	—	—	—	x	—
Date and place of death	—	—	o	o	—	—
Age at, and cause of, death	—	—	o	o	—	—

Key: x = annually or more often;
o = less often than annually, or once only;
— = not given.

Source: Sample data.

decade's directories, and use them to locate him in the next census. To facilitate tracing of sample members through the censuses, it behooves the researcher to run his sample members through a directory search as soon as he can.

Assessors' records, besides providing valuable economic data, may serve as surrogate city directories, for they contain names, addresses, and occupations, *arranged by streets*. They are thus extremely useful if one seeks data on, say, the occupational composition of neighborhoods. Even better, Boston's assessors started gathering this information, annually, long before any of it first appeared in a federal census (1850). One might, for instance, chart changes in Boston's economy on an annual basis by analyzing the ebb and flow of the city's labor force, as revealed in the assessors' books. Such analysis was of course beyond the scope of this study, which used the assessors' records only for the census years 1830, 1840, 1850, and 1860.

The Massachusetts State House contains the nation's oldest registration system, whose records date from 1841/42.[7] These are indexed by quinquennia, and the death records serve admirably to determine out-migration patterns from Boston for those fortunate enough to have died in Massachusetts. One may then backtrack them to the 1860, 1850, and/or 1840 census(es).

A possible alternative to the state registration system may offer itself in states where the system was set up too late to aid the ante-bellum researcher. An innovation of mid-nineteenth-century America, the suburban "garden" cemetery, was designed as an uncluttered resting place for those urbanites who could afford the entry fee. These cemeteries, assuming they still exist, maintain interment indices. After searching the indices of two large Boston area cemeteries the author would advise others to avoid these sources if they can, for the cemeteries' information about their clientele was more meager than that of the state registration system, while the number of sample members unearthed in the interment indices who had been missed by the state system was vanishingly small. Moreover, some cemeteries do not welcome inquisitive researchers who seek access to their interment indices.

Savings banks represent another source of richly detailed economic data which admirably supplements, even transcends, that of local tax records. In the present study, it proved impossible to get access to all the Boston banks' records, even for general statistical analyses. But other cities' banks may prove more co-operative.

We may now review briefly the kinds of information this study has collected, together with some of the limitations of that information. For each sample member this study sought to learn his place of birth, occupation, residences within Boston (and, where practicable, without), and economic achievement as measured by real and personal estate assessments in 1830, 1840, 1850, and 1860. This method produced four general *clusters* of information on most sample members: origins, occupation, residence, wealth. Since any of these clusters might be related to any other, the decision as to where to discuss reciprocal relationships was necessarily arbitrary.

As to limitations upon sample information, one should keep in mind the confidence level (95 per cent) and the confidence interval (plus or minus 5 per cent). A table of standard error for the estimated percentages appears as Appendix D. More important is that the sample refers to *heads of household.* Ordinarily, most were men. Adult males (over age 15) represented about one-third of Boston's population between 1830 and 1860; we have no guarantee that male heads of household were representative of all adult males. Too, the study did not collect data on sample members' wives, and their characteristics may diverge significantly from those of their husbands.

Utilizing most of the above sources, we may ask—and answer—quite a few questions concerning the plain people of ante-bellum Boston. Among these are: Where did they come from? What did they do for a living? How well did they do? Where did they live, and for how long? Where did they go when they left? With the *dramatis personae* in hand, it is time to view the stage before the actors tread it.

I

Prospects of Boston, 1830

We can scarcely take up a paper from any part of the Union, in which we do not find some indication of increasing prosperity. A strong, but gradual re-action has commenced, that promises to elevate us from the cheerless despondency of many years of constant and ominous retrocession.—Wherever we go, we find the most cheering evidence of the *goodness* of the times.

Boston *Daily Evening Transcript*,
7 October 1830, 2/2

By 1830 Boston was America's fourth largest city. Only New York (excluding Brooklyn), Philadelphia, and Baltimore were larger. Boston's 61,392 inhabitants lived on a peninsula; water restricted the city's growth, yet provided an avenue for coastal and international trade. There was warm-weather semi-weekly packet service to New York (three lines), Hartford, Albany, Portsmouth, and Dover (N.H.), and a boat every month to Charleston.[1] Clearings of 206,736 tons of vessels in the year ending 30 September 1830 ranked Boston third among the nation's ports, behind New York (548,336 tons) and New Orleans (260,970 tons).[2] By land, the city was said to have more stagecoaches running from it than from any other in the nation, with about 250 arrivals and departures a day.[3]

On its peninsula, the city grew in three ways: by simple outward extension to outlying areas, particularly to the south and across the harbor in East Boston; by infilling of shoreline; and by increasing density of population within its boundaries. Not till

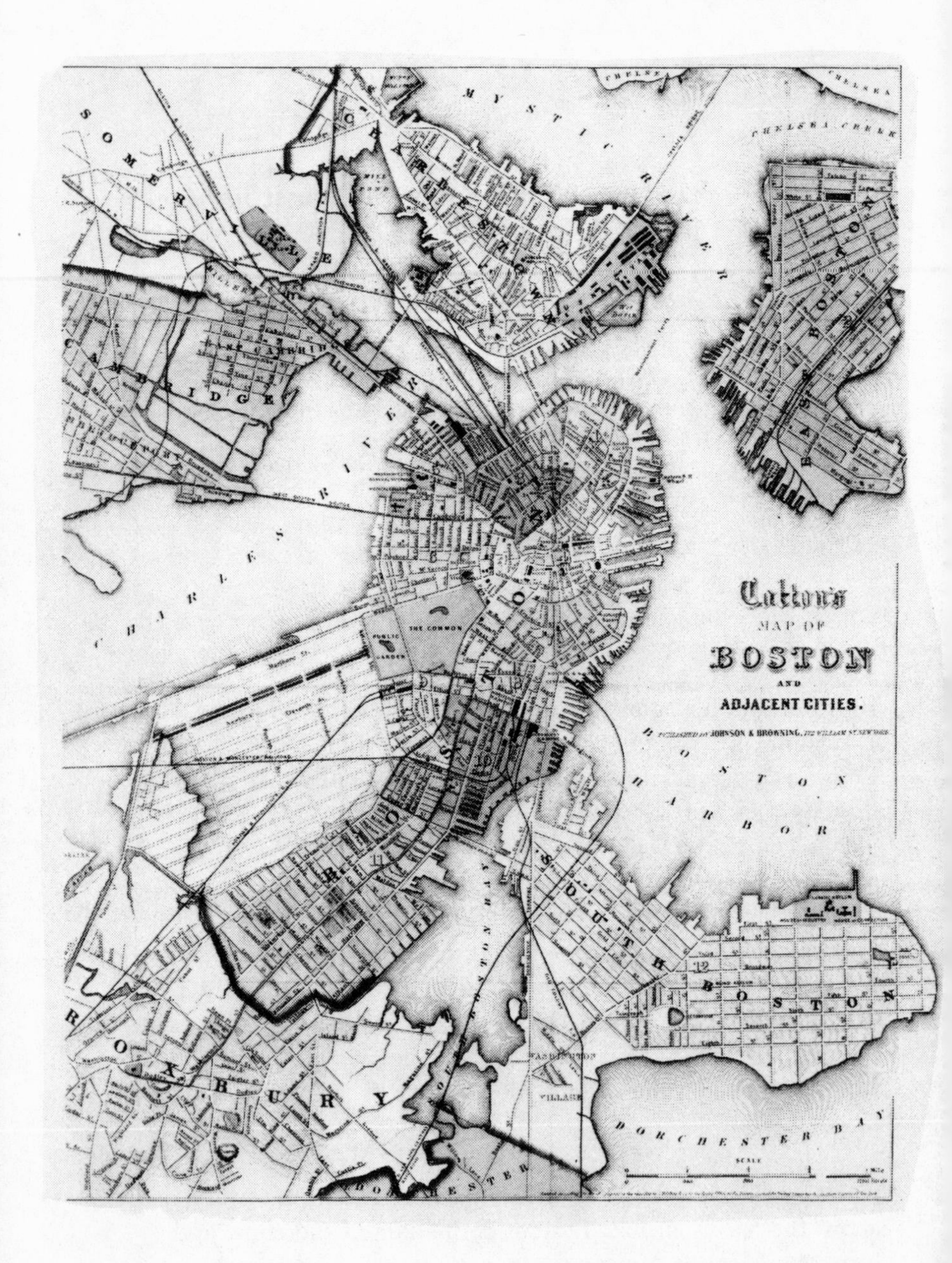
Colton's
MAP OF
BOSTON
AND
ADJACENT CITIES.
PUBLISHED BY JOHNSON & BROWNING, 172 WILLIAM ST. NEW YORK.
MYSTIC RIVER
CHELSEA CREEK
SOMERVILLE
CHARLESTOWN
EAST CAMBRIDGE
CAMBRIDGE
EAST BOSTON
CHARLES RIVER
THE COMMON
PUBLIC GARDEN
BOSTON HARBOR
SOUTH BOSTON
ROXBURY
WASHINGTON VILLAGE
DORCHESTER BAY
DORCHESTER
SCALE

after the Civil War did Boston annex any suburbs worth mentioning.[4]

In 1830 and immediately afterward, infilling occurred most heavily in two parts of the city: in the north end between the Charlestown and Craigie bridges, and in the Fort Point–South Channel area enclosed by the Free Bridge to South Boston (*cf.* Maps I and II). By 1838 the South Cove Corporation had advanced far enough with its filling operations that houses in the "New York streets" area began to be occupied, primarily by artisans and workers not chiefly engaged in dockside occupations. By contrast, the north end's filled-in area supported a population mostly dependent upon the docks, wharves, and shipyards of the north end.

The central area of Boston, said a contemporary,

> exhibits a noble appearance as the spectator sails up the harbor, or approaches it from the country. This splendid exterior, however, has not a corresponding regularity and symmetry within. The city was built almost from the beginning, without any regard to plan, beauty or future convenience, and the streets were left to fashion themselves into a tortuous intricacy that might have excited the envy of Daedalus of old.[5]

Because of the arrangement of its streets, Boston in 1830 consisted of five principal sections—exclusive of the central business district—which existed in relative isolation from one another. The north end of the city, bounded approximately by Leverett, Court, and State streets, contained persons chiefly engaged in maritime and riverine pursuits and food-marketing functions. The area to the west, known as West Boston or the west end, bounded by Leverett, Court, Washington, and Beacon streets, housed a good part of the city's independent artisans—masons and carpenters predominated. On the north side of Beacon Hill lay the city's Negro neighborhood, while on the south side there was a nascent neighborhood of clerks, artisans, merchants, and professional persons who walked over Pemberton Square down to the State Street–Court Street central business area.

South of the city's central business district lay a mixed business

RECEIVING BASIN
COMMON
Charles Street
Pleasant St
Washington Street
Front St
Buffalo
Albany
Hudson
Lincoln
Short St
Kingston
South Street
Broad Street
Federal
South Free Bridge
Turnpike St
S. B Iron Compy. Wf.
Boston Wf.
Plan of
SOUTH BOSTON.
Reduced from a drawing by
S. P. FULLER.
BOSTON HARBOUR
OLD HARBOUR
DORCHESTER
First
Second
Third
Broad
Fourth
Fifth
Sixth
Seventh
Eighth

CHARLES R.
Charles Street
George St.
Grove St.
Center St.
Bridge Street
Garden St.
Blossom Street
S. Russel St.
N. Russel St.
Belknap Street
Chamber St.
Hancock Street
Lynde St.
Leverett St.
Temple Street
Bowdoin Street
Somerset Street
Pemberton Square
Charlestown Street
Warren Bridge
South Part of BOSTON.
CHARLESTOWN
Ingersolls Wf.
Chamberlins Wf.
Thompson Wf.
Smiths Wf.
Bartletts Wf.
Gays Wf.
Comers Wf.
Fishers Wf.
Winnisimmet Ferry
Constitution Wf.
Union Wf.
T. Wharf
Long Wharf
Central Wharf
Commercial Street
Merchants Row
Custom House
Scale.

and residential area extending about to Summer Street. On the principal arteries—Washington, Congress, Kilby, and Broad streets—shops predominated in the immediate vicinity of State and Court streets, giving way after a couple of blocks to merchants' (particularly dry goods merchants') offices. On the "ring" streets north and south of the central business area, there clustered the city's boarding houses. Farther out, the "ring" streets contained a few stables and many private homes. The homes near High, Pearl, and Summer streets were monuments to successful merchants, who had a short stroll of two or three blocks to their wharfside offices.

South of Summer Street, the city was primarily residential, except for a line of shops extending down Washington Street more or less continuously to Kneeland Street. In quiet nooks off Washington Street stood the expensive houses of businessmen whose affairs centered upon the downtown business area rather than the harborside. South of the Common, there was abuilding a neighborhood of independent artisans similar to that of the northern section of the west end. Isolated from the city by distance lay South Boston, where relatively level land and city supervision permitted the imposition of a grid street pattern. Connected to the city proper only by bridges, South Boston's inhabitants, as they later complained,[6] had to fend for themselves, and developed some separatist feeling. As of 1830, the area supported an iron works, a glass factory, and several shipyards.

Communication patterns within the Boston of 1830 tended to reinforce, not diminish, neighborhood isolation. Probably the chief reason for this was the city's street pattern, with its paucity of radial streets and superabundance of ring streets:

> The Map is a perfect chaos, and all directions are set at defiance by the abrupt terminations of our high-ways, and their sinuous and uncertain windings. No one would take Boston as a model of a perfect City—no one would assume its devious paths as the true lines of civic beauty and convenience; yet no one has ever become thoroughly acquainted with the infinite variety and beauty of its hap-hazard streets, without feeling that the

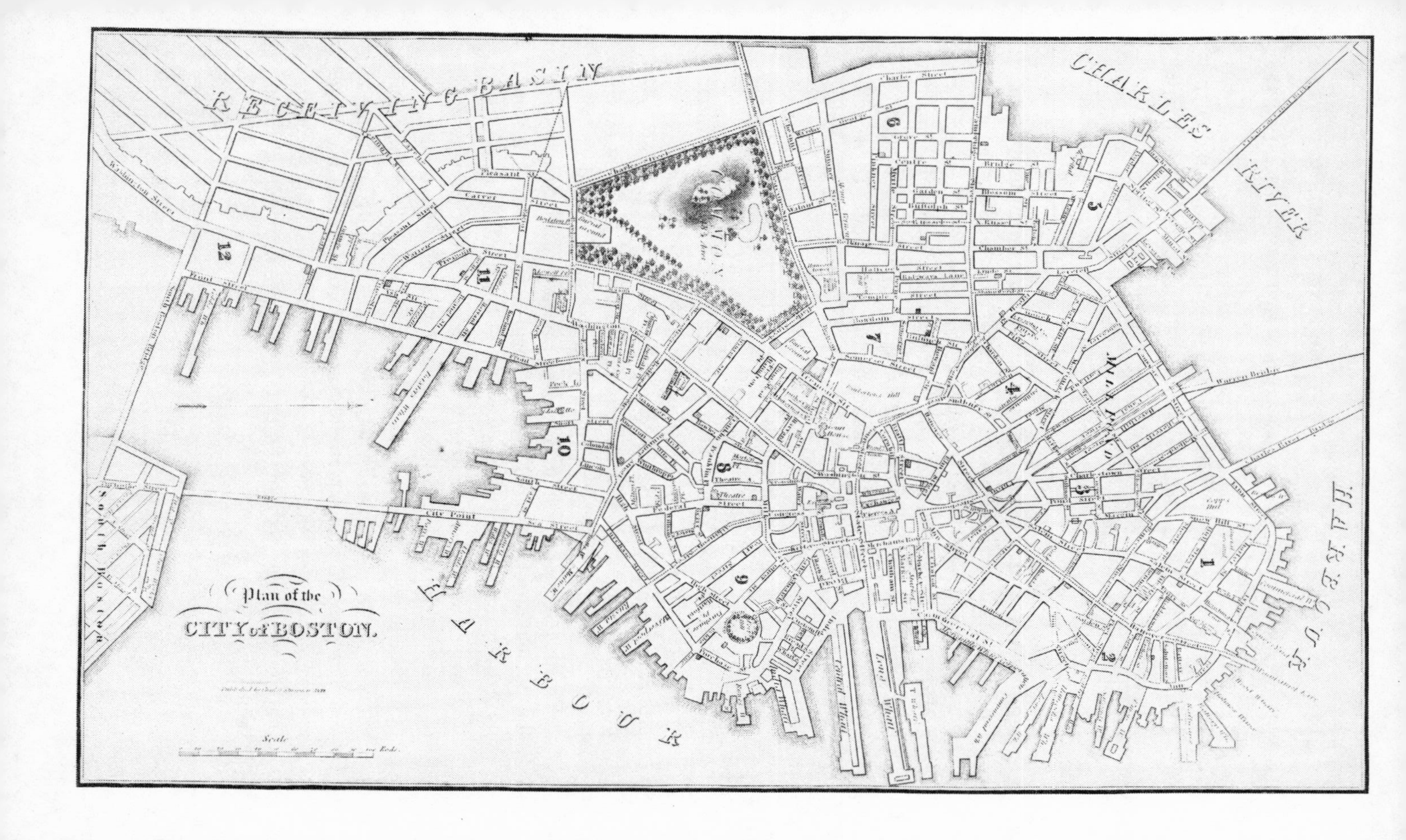

Plan of the
CITY of BOSTON
RECEIVING BASIN
CHARLES RIVER
HARBOUR
MILL POND
COMMON
South Boston
Scale
Long Wharf
Central Wharf
Charles Street
Pleasant St.
Carver
Front Street
Somerset Street
Bowdoin Street
Temple Street
Chamber St.
Centre St.
Grove St.
Charlestown Street
City Point
Sea Street
Warren Bridge
Charles River Bridge
Commercial St.
1
2
3
4
5
6
7
8
9
10
11
12

> fault of intricacy was more than repaid by the advantage of constant novelty.[7]

To walk from the city's north end to the west end involved detours around radial streets that did not penetrate to the city's heart. The section easiest of access from the central business district was that immediately to the south; it was the first to feel the pressure of increased housing densities in the 1840's.

Those seeking escape to the west faced the climb over Pemberton Square, or up Beacon Hill if they walked up Beacon Street, while the area south of Summer Street had only Washington Street as its thoroughfare to the city's center.

Visitors to Boston commented favorably upon its many churches and imposing public buildings, which ornament contemporary city guidebooks. From the dome of the new State House one could discern many of the features noted above, with the exception of residential preference patterns.

Yet the city of Boston consisted not only of streets, buildings, and wharves, but also of people. The hurrying throngs of State Street, Court Street, Washington Street, in their restless Brownian motion, remained largely neglected by visitors and residents alike, probably because of the throngs' very ubiquity. Besides, few persons were interested in the population *per se;* the only exceptions were the city assessors, making their annual rounds.

Except for the city's elite, who have been studied *ad nauseam,* the population of pre-Civil War Boston left few written personal records. Its monument was the city itself, which by the time of the Civil War was so completely torn apart and rebuilt that a resident of 1830 would have found few buildings, save churches and a few public buildings, remaining from his time. The influx, flux, and efflux of the city's people did not, however, go entirely unrecorded, and it is primarily from materials meant for ephemeral use, such as censuses, assessments, city directories, and vital statistics records, that some of the story of Boston's plain people may be reconstructed.

II

Population Trends in Boston, 1830–1860

> By the increase or decrease of the inhabitants, and by the changes in their number and proportions in the several parts of a country, we may, to some extent, judge of the state of all the other elements of society.
>
> JESSE CHICKERING[1]

> An autonomous social history ought to begin with a study of population: its changing composition and distribution in time and space.
>
> ERIC E. LAMPARD[2]

On Saturday, 6 September 1851, the police of Boston counted each person, carriage, cart, and train which entered or left the city between 6:30 a.m. and 7:30 p.m. During those thirteen hours, 41,729 persons entered Boston, while 42,313 left the city.[3] The city's population was then about 145,000; thus a group equal to about one-third of the population entered the city, and another, probably overlapping the first considerably, left the city. This statistic, representing part of Boston's commutation for just over half of one of the 11,000 days from 1830 to 1860, emphasizes anew the fragility of the concept of a city's "population."

Again, the federal census of Boston for 1850, taken as of 1 June, did not get under way until 1 August (Ward 9). The tardiest start was 30 September (Ward 11), by which time the enumerators in Ward 8 had been finished for twelve days. The enumerators for Wards 6 and 7 finished on 11 October.[4] Thus the information "as of 1 June" was actually collected between 1 August and 11 October, from two to a little more than four months later (*cf.* Appendix C for an effect of this tardiness).

A statement such as "Boston's population as of 1 June 1850 was 136,881," should consequently call to mind the constant fluctuation of individuals composing the city, as well as the fact that censuses provide, at best, approximations of population enumerations. Accordingly, city population figures in this study will often be rounded to the nearest hundred, while percentages may be rounded to the nearest full per cent.

From 1830 to 1860, Boston experienced a net population growth of 116,400, or an average of just over ten per day. The total population almost tripled (Table II-1).

Table II-1. Population Growth of Boston, 1820-1860

Year	*Population (thousands)*	*Per cent Gain in Population*		
		Over past		
		Five Years	*Ten Years*	*Over 1830*
1820	43.3	n.a.	28	–
1825	58.3	5	n.a.	–
1830	61.4	5	35	–
1835	78.6	28	35	28
(1837)	80.8	n.a.	n.a.	32
1840	84.4	8	38	38
1845	114.4	35	47	86
1850	136.9	20	61	123
1855	161.4	16	41	163
1860	177.8	10	30	190

n.a. – not available

Sources: For censuses of 1820, 1825, 1830, 1835, 1840, 1845: Lemuel Shattuck, *Report to the Committee of the City Council Appointed to Obtain the Census of Boston for the Year 1845 . . .* (Boston: John H. Eastburn, 1846), Appendix 12-Appendix 17; for the census of 1837, Boston City Document No. 20 (1838), 5-10; for the censuses of 1850 and 1855, *Report of the Joint Special Committee on the Census of Boston, May, 1855,. . . .* (Boston: Moore & Crosby, 1856), 7-8; for the census of 1860, Massachusetts. Secretary of the Commonwealth, *Abstract of the Census of Massachusetts, 1860, from the Eighth U. S. Census, with Remarks on the Same . . .* (Boston: Wright & Potter, 1863), 46.

Both relatively and absolutely Boston's ante-bellum growth ranked high among the nation's cities (Tables II-2 and II-3), and

Table II-2. Relative Population Growth and Rank Order of the Ten Largest Cities of 1830, United States, 1830-1860

City	*1830 Rank*	*1830 Population (thousands)*	*1860 Population (thousands)*	*1860 Rank*	*Per Cent Gain 1830-1860*
Cincinnati	7	24.8	161.0	7	549
New Orleans	6	29.7	168.7	6	468
New York	1	197.1	805.7	1	309
Washington	9	18.8	61.1	14	225
Providence	10	16.8	50.7	16	202
Philadelphia (County)*	2	188.8	565.5	2	200
BOSTON	4	61.4	177.8	5	190
Baltimore	3	80.6	212.4	4	164
Albany	8	24.2	62.4	13	158
Charleston	5	30.3	40.5	22	34

*For comparability, Philadelphia's 1830 population has been increased to include as well that of Philadelphia County, annexed in 1854.

Source: U. S. Bureau of the Census, *Compendium of the Eleventh Census: 1890. Part I.—Population.* (Washington: Government Printing Office, 1892), 434-37.

was in some ways perhaps the more remarkable because of Boston's small area as compared with that of most other major cities. While Boston was advancing 190 per cent in population between 1830 and 1860, the nation grew by 143 per cent. In contrast, all "urban places" (over 2500 population) moved up 464 per cent; places under 2500 grew by only 115 per cent.[5] Boston's growth rate was rather nearer that of the nation than that of urban places.

Within New England, Boston's position as the largest city was never really in doubt; Portland, Providence, and New Haven did not threaten it. After 1840 there occurred a sharp increase in the growth rates of the southern New England states (see Table III-4). Southern New England was urbanizing rapidly in the early nine-

Table II-3. Ten Cities Having Largest Absolute Population Growth, United States, 1830-1860

City	*1830 Rank*	*1830 Population (thousands)*	*1860 Population (thousands)*	*1860 Rank*	*Population Growth 1830-1860 (thousands)*
New York	1	197.1	805.7	1	608.6
Philadelphia (County)*	2	188.8	565.5	2	376.7
Brooklyn**	16	12.4	266.7	3	254.3
St. Louis**	12	14.1	160.8	8	146.7
New Orleans	6	29.7	168.7	6	139.0
Cincinnati	7	24.8	161.0	7	136.2
Baltimore	3	80.6	212.4	4	131.8
BOSTON	4	61.4	177.8	5	116.4
Chicago**	–	–	109.3	9	109.3
Buffalo**	23	8.7	81.1	10	72.4

* For comparability, Philadelphia's 1830 population has been increased to include as well that of Philadelphia County, annexed in 1854.
**Not listed in Table II-2.

Source: U. S. Bureau of the Census, *Compendium of the Eleventh Census: 1890. Part I.—Population.* (Washington: Government Printing Office, 1892), 434-37.

teenth century. Where in 1810 there had been only three towns in the area with populations over 10,000, containing 6.9 per cent of the three states' population, by 1840 nine towns over 10,000 held 18.5 per cent of the population. As of 1860, 26 towns qualified in the 10,000 and over category; they contained 36.5 per cent of the three states' inhabitants.[6]

Within Massachusetts, according to Jesse Chickering, a pioneer statistician, the centralization of population antedated 1810, for

> During the twenty-five years from 1765 to 1790, the increase of the population was greater in parts distant from Boston; but during the fifty years from the first census of the United States [1790], it was greater *in* and *near* Boston, showing a tendency to a centralization of the population in and near the capital of the Commonwealth.[7]

This trend continued through 1860 (see Table II-4). By 1865,

Table II-4. Proportion of the Population of Boston and Vicinity to That of Massachusetts, 1830-1860

Area	*Proportion (%) of Massachusetts' Population*			
	1830	*1840*	*1850*	*1860*
Boston	10.1	12.7	13.8	14.4
Towns Contiguous to Boston	4.4	5.3	7.5	10.1
Non-contiguous Towns within 10 Miles of Boston	5.0	5.5	6.3	7.4
Totals	19.5	23.5	27.6	31.9

Sources: Jesse Chickering, *A Statistical View of the Population of Massachusetts, from 1765 to 1840* (Boston: Charles C. Little & James Brown, 1846), 54, 63; Massachusetts. Secretary of the Commonwealth, *Abstract of the Census of Massachusetts, 1860,* 201-11.

said the Secretary of the Commonwealth in his report on the state census of that year, Massachusetts' center of population lay about two miles southwest of the State House.[8]

To judge from the various censuses of ante-bellum Boston, reported population changes within the city were confusing and often contradictory. The variations may be an artifact of the remarkable residential mobility of ante-bellum Bostonians, discussed in Chapter IV. Since it is impossible to "go behind the returns," they must be approached with some caution. As early as 1846, Lemuel Shattuck was aware of these shortcomings: "In a City population of a fluctuating character, and of locomotive habits, like that of Boston, these difficulties are far greater than in the more stationary population of the country."[9] Shattuck noted an "apparent irregular growth of the City," which, extended throughout the period of study, appears in Table II-5. Although this phenomenon of marked disparity in intercensal growth rates becomes less noticeable after 1845, Shattuck, who first noted it, and who was more than a century closer to it in time, concluded that "On the supposition that these several enumerations were all

Table II-5. Differential Growth Rates in Census Intervals, 1820-1865: City-National *versus* National-City

Census Interval	*Per cent Growth in Intervals Between City and National Censuses*	*Per cent Growth in Intervals Between National and City Censuses*
1820–25		34.6
1825–30	5.3	
1830–35		28.0
1835–40	8.1	
1840–45		34.5
1845–50	21.4	
1850–55		16.3
1855–60	10.3	
1860–65		8.2

Source: Same as Table II-1.

accurately made; and that the National censuses of 1820 and 1830 were not too low, nor the City census [*sic*] of 1825 and 1835 too high, it is difficult to account for this apparent irregular growth of the city." [10] At the ward level, the situation was also disparate (see Table II-6). That the disparity is an artifact of the sponsorship of adjacent censuses shows more clearly in Table II-7, which contrasts alternate censuses taken by the same authorities. The more evenly balanced distribution of population losses apparent in Table II-7, as against those in Table II-6, suggests that the city censuses were more nearly inclusive of the "real" population than were the national censuses.

Even with the handicap of erratic censuses, one may distinguish several major features of Boston's maturing in the ante-bellum period. Up to 1835, all of the city's wards gained inhabitants; thereafter, some began losing them. Beginning about 1845, the preponderance of peripheral over central city growth became quite marked, as the central area stagnated and then retrogressed (in terms of population only). During this latter process, adult

Table II-6. Number of Boston's Wards Losing Population in Census Intervals, 1825-1865: City-National *versus* National-City

Census Interval	*Number of Wards Losing Population in Intervals Between City and National Censuses*	*Number of Wards Losing Population in Intervals Between National and City Censuses*
1825-30	3	
1830-35		0
1837*-40	3	
1840-45		0
1845-50	3	
1850-55		1
1855-60	5	
1860-65		4

*There was a special city census, for redistricting of the wards, in 1837; since ward boundaries were changed in 1838, the 1835 and 1840 census figures are not comparable, but those for 1837 and 1840 are.

Sources: For censuses of 1820, 1825, 1830, 1835, 1840, 1845: Lemuel Shattuck, *Report to the Committee of the City Council,* Appendix 12-Appendix 17; for the census of 1837, *Boston City Document No. 20* (1838), 5-10; for the censuses of 1850 and 1855, *Report of the Joint Special Committee on the Census of Boston, May, 1855,* 7-8; for the census of 1860, Massachusetts. Secretary of the Commonwealth, *Abstract of the Census of Massachusetts, 1860,* 46.

females finally gained a plurality over adult males in the central wards, accompanying the plurality they had held in peripheral wards since at least 1825.

Before proceeding to the detailed exposition of gross population trends within Boston, the reader may wish to look at the maps, which show "central" and "peripheral" areas as defined by the ward boundaries of 1822–38, 1838–50, and 1850–66. The ward boundary revisions of 1838 and 1850 divide Boston's ante-bellum censuses into three non-comparable groups: 1825 (for trend analysis), 1830, 1835, and 1837 (old ward limits); 1837 (new wards), 1840, 1845, and 1850 (old ward boundaries); and 1850 (new ward divisions), 1855, 1860, and 1865 (for trends). For pur-

Table II-7. Number of Boston's Wards Losing Population During Census Intervals, 1825-1865: City-City *versus* National-National

Census Interval	*Number of Wards Losing Population in Intervals Between City Censuses*	*Number of Wards Losing Population in Intervals Between National Censuses*
1825-35	0	
1830-40		not comparable; city redistricted
1835-37	3	
1840-50		1
1837-45	1	
1850-60		2
1845-55	not comparable; city redistricted	
1855-65	5	

Source: Same as Table II-1.

poses of analysis, the city's central area has been defined as Ward 4 (always the central business district) and all contiguous wards. The peripheral area consists of the rest of the wards.

Throughout the period 1825–65, with the possible exception of 1837–40, population growth rates of Boston's peripheral wards consistently outstripped those of the central wards. A few relative and absolute growth figures for central and peripheral areas appear in Table II-8. Not only did the peripheral wards grow faster than the central wards, they accelerated more rapidly also, from a percentage gain of about one and a half times that of the central wards in 1825–37, to four times as much in 1837–50, and about forty times as much in 1850–65 (column 4 in Table II-8). In absolute terms, the periphery contributed about twice as much as did the center in the first period, roughly three times as much in the second, and about thirty-nine times as much in the last (column 5 in Table II-8).

During 1830–35, all the city's wards gained population, the southern wards (9, 11, 12) most of all. It was between 1835 and

Table II-8. "Central" and "Peripheral" Population Changes in Boston, 1825-1837, 1837-1850, and 1850-1865[a]

	1. *1825 Population*	2. *1837 Population*	3. *Net Gain [(2)–(1)]*	4. Net Gain as *% of (1)*	5. *Net Gain as % of City Gain*
Center	25,101	32,210	7,109	28.3	31.5
Periphery	33,176	48,613	15,437	46.5	68.5
City	58,277	80,823	22,546	38.7	100.0
	1. *1837 Population*	2. *1850 Population*			
Center	46,221	60,647	14,426	31.2	24.9
Periphery	34,602	78,141	43,539	125.8	75.1
City	80,823	138,788	57,965	71.7	100.0
	1. *1850 Population*	2. *1865 Population*			
Center	74,279	75,688	1,409	1.9	2.6
Periphery	64,509	116,630	52,121	80.8	97.4
City	138,788	192,318	53,530	38.6	100.0

[a] Boston's wards were redistricted in 1838, 1850, and 1866; just before each redistricting, a census of the city was taken. The differing figures above for 1837 and 1850 reflect the redistricting. For definitions of "center" and "periphery," see the accompanying text.

Sources: 1825, Lemuel Shattuck, *Report to the Committee of the City Council,* Appendix 13; 1837, *Boston City Document No. 20* (1838), 5-10; 1850, *Boston City Document No. 42* (1850), 30; 1865, Massachusetts. Secretary of the Commonwealth, *Abstract of the Census of Massachusetts, 1865: With Remarks on the Same, ...* (Boston: Wright & Potter, 1867), 44.

1837 that the city's growth apparently paused momentarily, for Wards 7, 8, 9, and 11 registered population losses, while the city as a whole advanced only 2.8 per cent. Most of the gain in the central area's growth resulted from a net inflow of adult males, who generally outnumbered adult females about 110 or 120 to 100 in the central area. Peripheral growth during 1825–37 resulted largely from a net increase there of children and adult women. The latter usually outnumbered adult men in the peripheral wards about 105 up to 120 per 100.

Between 1837 and 1840 (after the ward redistricting of 1838), the city grew about 5 per cent, with Ward 2 leading the way at

24.1 per cent. With the exceptions of Wards 1 (+10.0%) and 6 (+9.8%), most wards barely held their own. Population loss first appeared in the central business district (Ward 4, −2.6%; Ward 7, −5.0%). From 1840 to 1850, peripheral growth, at the expense of central, became rampant. East and South Boston flourished (+602% and +115%, respectively). This growth had been anticipated by the City Council in its ward redistricting of 1838, for it then set off South Boston as a separate ward (12), and yoked East Boston with the central business district in Ward 4, intending thereby to compensate for population losses in the business area.[11] There was no doubt that the business area was expanding at the expense of residential housing: Ward 2 gained but one per cent in the 1840's, while Ward 7 lost 18.3 per cent. Notwithstanding the tearing down of some dwellings in central areas, Shattuck noted in 1845 that population continued to increase in the area north of Boylston and Beach streets because of "doubling up," with densities of 121 persons per acre in 1840 and 143 in 1845, an increase of 18 per cent in just five years.[12]

In late 1850, the City Council again rearranged ward lines, but on the basis of the number of voters rather than of inhabitants (Handlin claims this aimed to minimize the voting impact of Irish immigrants[13]). The 'fifties witnessed a continuation of trends of the later 'forties. After 1845, in the central area the ratio of adult males per 100 adult females first fell below 100, to 95 (1850, old ward limits), 93 (1850, new boundaries), to 94 in 1855, and to 91 in 1860, indicating a progressive displacement of adult males by adult females. After 1845, as previously noted, the whole city finally exhibited a plurality of adult females. In the 'fifties, central areas either lost considerably (Ward 4, −17.8%; Ward 7, −10.2%), or stagnated (between 1855 and 1860, Ward 5 lost three inhabitants and Ward 6, twelve). In the south, Wards 12 (South Boston) and 11 nearly doubled, as did Ward 2 (East Boston). The city's center reached a population plateau and began to decline, while the periphery provided all the city's net population gains.

Two other prominent population characteristics are those of race, and household or family size. (The latter will not be discussed in this study, as no clear-cut patterns emerged from its analysis.) Boston's Negroes never constituted more than about 3 per cent of the city's population* during the three ante-bellum

Table II-9. Negro Population as Per Cent of Boston's Population, 1825-1865

Year	City Population (Thousands)	Per Cent Gain in 5 Years	Negro Population	Per Cent Change in 5 Years	Negro Population as Per Cent of City Population
1825	58.3	5	191	10.3	3.3
1830	61.4	5	1875	–2.3	3.1
1835	78.6	28	1757	–6.1	2.2
1840	84.4	8	1988	13.3	2.4
1845	114.4	35	1842	–7.9	1.6
1850	136.9	20	1999	8.0	1.5
1855	161.4	16	2216	10.8	1.4
1860	177.8	10	2261	2.1	1.3
1865	192.3	8	2333	3.2	1.2

Sources: Lemuel Shattuck, *Report to the Committee of the City Council,* 43; U. S. Census Office. Seventh Census (1850), *The Seventh Census of the United States: 1850. . . .* (Washington: Robert Armstrong, 1853), 52; *Report of the Joint Special Committee on the Census of Boston, May, 1855,* 7; Massachusetts. Secretary of the Commonwealth, *Abstract of the Census of Massachusetts, 1860,* 106 (eliminating 23 Indians); Massachusetts. Secretary of the Commonwealth, *Abstract of the Census of Massachusetts, 1865,* 118 (eliminating 15 Indians); total city population figures are from Table II-1.

decades; their proportion of the population dwindled steadily (see Table II-9). Only during 1825–30 and 1835–40 did they increase more rapidly than the whites. Jesse Chickering concluded in 1846 that Boston's Negro population had increased between 1830 and 1840 only because of immigration.[14] Further, he said,

> A prejudice has existed in the community, and still exists against them on account of their color, and on account of their being the descendants of slaves. They cannot obtain employment on equal terms with the whites, and wherever they go a sneer is passed upon them, as if this sportive inhumanity were an act of

* Of the 1,540 sample members, 44 (2.9 per cent) were Negroes.

> merit. . . . Thus, though their legal rights are the same as those of whites, their condition is one of degradation and dependence. . . .[15]

Between 1830 and 1860, Boston contained from one-quarter to one-fifth of the state's Negroes. This proportion reached its minimum in 1850 and began rising. The slight relative outflow of Negroes to other towns in the state reversed itself sometime between 1840 and 1855 (see Table II-10).

Table II-10. Boston's Proportion of Massachusetts' Negroes, 1820-1865

Census	*Boston's Negroes*	*Negroes in Massachusetts*	*Boston's Proportion (Per Cent) of State's Total Negroes*
1820 (Federal)	1740	6740	25.8
1830 (Federal)	1875	7045	26.6
1840 (Federal)	1988	8669	22.9
1850 (Federal)	1999	9064	22.1
1855 (State)	2216	9777	22.7
1860 (Federal)	2261	9602	23.5
1865 (State)	2333	10,167	22.9

Sources: Lemuel Shattuck, *Report to the Committee of the City Council,* 43; Table II-9; Jesse Chickering, *A Statistical View of the Population of Massachusetts, from 1765 to 1840.,* 122; Massachusetts. Secretary of the Commonwealth, *Abstract of the Census of the Commonwealth of Massachusetts, Taken with Reference to Facts Existing on the First Day of June, 1855. With Remarks on the Same.* (Boston: William White, 1857), 63 (eliminating 139 Indians); U. S. Census Office. Eighth Census (1860), *Population of the United States in 1860;. . . .* (Washington: Government Printing Office, 1864), 220; Massachusetts. Secretary of the Commonwealth, *Abstract of the Census of Massachusetts, 1865,* 231, 234 (eliminating 15 Indians).

Boston's Negroes concentrated in the northern part of the city, particularly on the north side of Beacon Hill (always in Ward 6) and in the streets to the north of Cambridge Street (always in Ward 5). The proportion of Negroes living in the four wards having the largest numbers of Negroes rose generally during the antebellum period, indicating increasing segregation of the Negro population (Table II-11). Considerable shifting of the Negro pop-

Table II-11. Negro Population in Boston's Four Wards with Largest Negro Population as Per Cent of City's Negro Population, 1825-1865

Year	1. *Negroes in Four Wards with Largest Negro Populations*	2. *Total Negroes in City*	3. *(1) as Per Cent of (2)*	*Wards with Largest Negro Populations*
1825	1429	1917	74.5	2, 5, 6, 7
1830	1433	1875	76.4	2, 5, 6, 7
1835	1414	1757	80.5	2, 5, 6, 7
1840	1692	1988	85.1	1, 2, 5, 6
1845	n. a.	1842	n. a.	n. a.
1850 (Federal)	1675	1999	83.8	1, 2, 5, 6
1850 (City)	1708 (old Wards)	2085	81.9	2, 5, 6, 11
1850 (City)	1792 (new Wards)	2085	85.9	1, 5, 6, 11
1855	1859	2216	83.9	1, 5, 6, 11
1860	1933	2261	85.5	1, 3, 5, 6
1865	2048	2333	87.8	1, 5, 6, 11

n. a. — not available.

Sources: Lemuel Shattuck, *Report to the Committee of the City Council,* Appendix 13-Appendix 15, Appendix 17; U. S. Census Office. Seventh Census (1850), *The Seventh Census of the United States: 1850,* 52; *Boston City Document No. 42* (1850), 30; *Report of the Joint Special Committee on the Census of Boston, May, 1855,* 7; U. S. Census Office. Eighth Census (1860), *Population of the United States in 1860,* 225; Massachusetts. Secretary of the Commonwealth, *Abstract of the Census of Massachusetts, 1865,* 118, 120.

ulation into already settled Negro areas continued through the Civil War; by 1865, only 285 Negroes lived outside the four most densely occupied "Negro" wards.

Central-peripheral distribution comparisons for the Negroes do not work out well because the change of ward limits in 1838 made Ward 6 (Beacon Hill area) contiguous with Ward 4, changing Ward 6 from a peripheral to a central ward (as defined above). Since Ward 6 usually contained about 60 per cent of the city's

Negroes, this shifted the central wards' proportion of Negroes from 29.9 per cent in 1835 to 86.6 per cent in 1840! If, however, we look at the periods before and after 1840, there is evident a marked shift of Negroes to peripheral wards in 1825–35 (1825, 56.4%; 1830, 68.7%; 1835, 70.1%). But from 1840 to 1865 the proportion of Negroes in the central wards hovered around 85 per cent. The outward stream of Negroes stopped, and proportions stabilized after 1840. Negroes thus did not participate in the general outward movement of population from the central business district that occurred after about 1845. Since their jobs were menial, and menial or casual jobs tended to concentrate near the central business district, Negroes probably tended to remain there also. Too, popular feeling against them may have kept them from moving into previously white areas.

Having determined to some extent the gross population movements within the state and the city, as background to the particularistic study of sample members, we may proceed to an examination of findings based on the sample itself. The sampling method here demonstrates one of its great advantages over the review of statistical trends (such as that of this chapter): while statistical comparisons are like periodic checking account balances, the sampling method allows us to follow transactions themselves. We may then gain a better notion of what occurred in, say, population shifts. Were the people who participated in the shift from central to peripheral wards the same persons who had lived in the central wards? Or did people tend to remain in a neighborhood, so that peripheral growth resulted from an excess of peripheral in-migrants over central in-migrants? Before attempting to examine these questions it would be as well to learn where Boston's people came from, since this may bear on where they lived and where they went.

III

Sources of Boston's Population

The birth places of a population are quite interesting and important.

LEMUEL SHATTUCK[1]

In a place like Boston it is exceedingly difficult, [even] with all the helps its officers can give, to trace out the parentage and history of the foreign poor. There are so many John Sullivans, Jerry Daileys and William O'Briens, who are all made in the same mould, ...

JOHN G. LOCKE,
Agent of the Alien Commissioners[2]

Where did Boston's people come from? Not until the city census of 1845 did census takers ask Bostonians where they had been born. But the federal census of 1830 counted the total of aliens (i.e., non-citizens) in each household. Boston contained 3468 aliens, 5.6 per cent of the city's total population. Presumably most of the remaining 94.4 per cent were native-born. The 1845 city census distinguished only persons born in Boston, born in the United States outside Boston, and born abroad.[3] By 1845, the "foreign element" had increased to 23.7 per cent of the population; their children amounted to another 8.9 per cent, a total of 32.6 per cent. Native Bostonians made up 35.9 per cent of the population, or 27.0 per cent with the subtraction of foreigners' children. Other Americans constituted 40.4 per cent of the city's population.[4]

The federal census of 1850 was the first to inquire into *state* of birth. That census revealed three principal population components in mid-century Boston: natives of Massachusetts (including foreigners' children), 50.7 per cent; Irish, 26.0 per cent; and persons born in the other five New England states, 12.6 per cent.[5] The state census of 1855 subdivided foreign birthplaces by country, but lumped together as native Americans all persons born in the United States, including foreigners' children. Of the city's 160,271 classified residents in 1855, 61.1 per cent were native-born, down 4.5 percentage points from 1850. Of the 38.9 per cent foreign-born, 28.8 per cent were Irish, a gain of 2.8 percentage points.[6]

By 1860 there seems to have been an outflow of foreign-born, or a strong inward stream of natives, or perhaps a moderate combination thereof, for Massachusetts natives (including foreigners' children) constituted 48.7 per cent of Boston's inhabitants, other New Englanders 12.3 per cent, and the total for all "Americans" amounted to 64.1 per cent, a rise of 3.0 percentage points in five years, or just 1.5 percentage points less than in 1850. Ireland's proportion had fallen off to 25.9 per cent, a loss of 2.9 percentage points in five years and 0.1 point for the decade.[7]

This apparent reversal of a trend toward an increasingly Irish city was illusory if one regarded cultural backgrounds closely, for an important fraction of Boston's population was that of persons under 21. The city censuses of 1845 and 1855 and the state census of 1850 all classified as "foreign" those aged under 21 who had foreign parents, for "subject as they are to the control, instruction, and associations of their parents, they properly belong to, and are under the influence of the foreign element." [8] Accepting this definition of "foreign" results in the trend shown on the right-hand side of Table III-1. Between 1856 and 1859, the percentage of children reported born in Boston to Irish-born parents ranged between 46.4 and 48.6, and the spread of percentages where both parents were foreigners was from 59.3 to 64.6, so that up to 1860, at least, the proportion of children in the city born of foreign parents probably continued to rise.[9] The apparent reversal, while demographically correct, was not culturally so, at least as defined by ante-bellum Boston's standards.

This chapter will focus exclusively upon birthplace information

Table III-1. "Native" and "Foreign" Population of Boston According to Various Definitions of "Foreign," 1845-1865 (Per Cent)

Year	*By Place of Birth*		*Born in United States of Foreign Parentage*	*By Parentage*	
	Native	*Foreign*		*Native*	*Foreign*
1845	76.3	23.7	8.9	67.4	32.6
1850	65.6	34.4	11.3	54.3	45.7
1855	61.1	38.9	14.1	47.0	53.0
1860	64.1	35.9	n.a.	n.a.	n.a.
1865	65.8	34.2	n.a.	n.a.	n.a.

n.a. — not available

Sources: Lemuel Shattuck, *Report to the Committee of the City Council Appointed to Obtain the Census of Boston for the Year 1845,* . . . . (Boston: John H. Eastburn, 1846), Appendix 20; U. S. Census Office. Seventh Census (1850), *Statistical View of the United States, . . . A Compendium of the Seventh Census. . . .* (Washington: A. O. P. Nicholson, 1854), 399; *Boston City Document No. 42* (1850), 30; Massachusetts. Secretary of the Commonwealth, *Abstract of the Census of the Commonwealth of Massachusetts, . . . June, 1855. . . .* (Boston: Moore & Crosby, 1856), 7; U. S. Census Office. Eighth Census (1860), *Population of the United States in 1860;. . . .* (Washington: Government Printing Office, 1864), 608; Massachusetts. Secretary of the Commonwealth, *Abstract of the Census of Massachusetts, 1865: With Remarks. . . .* (Boston: Wright & Potter, 1867), 76.

for Bostonians, leaving possible connections of birthplace with residence, occupation, or wealth to later chapters. Sample results for heads of households appear in Table III-2. Not all members of the 1830 and 1840 samples could be traced as far back as their birthplaces; hence the percentages for those two samples are based on the number of persons of known background.

Several trends appear in the distribution of sample members' birthplaces. Particularly evident is the relative decline in representation of persons born in the outlying or "outstate" towns of Massachusetts. The proportion of Boston-born sample members fell off nearly one-half. From 1840 to 1860, the fraction of sample members born in outstate Massachusetts declined to a little less than one-quarter of what it had been, while the proportion of sample members from the other five New England states increased about one-third (see Table III-3).

Table III-2. Distribution, by Per Cent, of Sample Members' Birthplaces, 1830, 1840, 1850, 1860

State or Country of Birth	*Per Cent of Sample Born in That State or Country*			
	1830	*1840*	*1850*	*1860*
Massachusetts	63.9	57.8	32.2	22.9
New Hampshire	8.8	7.9	8.3	7.5
Maine	2.8	5.1	6.2	8.8
Vermont	1.4	2.2	2.9	2.1
Connecticut	1.4	1.1	0.5	0.5
Rhode Island	–	0.4	0.3	–
New England Total	78.7	74.3	50.4	42.1
New York and New Jersey	–	0.4	1.3	1.3
Maryland, Virginia, and District of Columbia	1.0	0.8	0.3	1.0
Other United States	–	–	0.3	–
Total United States	79.6	75.4	52.2	44.4
Ireland	17.1	18.1	37.7	41.8
England (only)	2.3	2.9	3.6	2.1
Scotland	–	0.7	2.1	1.8
Germany, Holland, Sweden, Poland, and Switzerland	–	1.1	2.1	3.4
France, Spain, and Italy	–	0.7	0.5	0.3
Brazil	0.5	–	–	–
Canada (modern area)	0.5	1.1	1.3	6.2
Total foreign	20.4	24.6	47.3	55.6
Unknown (so listed in census)	–	–	0.5	–
Number of sample members of known birthplace (equals 100 per cent)	216	277	385	385
Birthplace not determined	169	108	–	–

Source: Sample data. Totals may not add because of rounding.

Table III-3. Proportions, by Per Cent, of Sample Members Born in Boston, Outside Boston but in Massachusetts, in Massachusetts but Specific Location Unknown, and in the Other Five New England States, 1830, 1840, 1850, 1860

Area or Place of Birth	*Per Cent of Sample Born in That Area or Place*			
	1830	*1840*	*1850*	*1860*
Boston	16.7	17.3	10.4	10.7
Outside Boston but in Massachusetts	44.0	37.9	17.7	9.9
Massachusetts, no specific location	3.2	2.5	3.9	2.3
Total Massachusetts	63.9	57.8	32.0	22.9
Other Five New England States	14.8	16.3	18.4	19.2
Number of sample members of known birthplace (equals 100 per cent)	216	277	385	385

Source: Sample data. Totals may not add because of rounding.

These population shifts formed part of larger movements occurring within Massachusetts and New England (see Table III-4). Those areas growing most quickly were also "urbanizing" (i.e., attaining populated places of over 2500) fastest (see Table III-5). By 1860, seven out of ten persons in southern New England (Massachusetts, Connecticut, and Rhode Island) lived in places of over 2500 population, while seven out of ten persons in northern New England (Vermont, New Hampshire, and Maine) lived in places of under 2500 population. As for specific components of the population, northern New England, which was not growing as quickly as southern, manifested three characteristics: relative out-migration of individuals born in northern New England, lower rates of in-migration of native-born from other states to northern New England, and lower rates of immigration to northern New England by

Table III-4. Populations (in Thousands) and Growth Rates of the New England States, 1820-1860

State or Area	*1820 Population (x 1000)*	*Growth 1820-1830 (%)*	*1830 Population (x 1000)*	*Growth 1830-1840 (%)*	*1840 Population (x 1000)*	*Growth 1840-1850 (%)*	*1850 Population (x 1000)*	*Growth 1850-1860 (%)*	*1860 Population (x 1000)*
Maine	298.3	33.9	399.5	25.6	501.8	16.2	583.2	7.7	628.3
New Hampshire	244.0	10.3	269.3	5.7	284.6	11.7	318.0	2.6	326.1
Vermont	235.7	19.0	280.7	4.0	291.9	7.6	314.1	0.3	315.1
Northern New England	778.0	22.1	949.5	13.5	1078.3	12.7	1215.3	4.5	1269.5
MASSACHUSETTS	523.2	16.7	610.4	20.9	737.7	34.8	994.5	23.8	1231.1
Rhode Island	83.0	17.6	97.2	12.0	108.8	35.6	147.5	18.4	174.6
Connecticut	275.1	8.2	297.7	4.1	310.0	19.6	370.8	24.1	460.1
Southern New England	881.3	14.1	1005.3	15.0	1156.5	30.8	1512.8	23.5	1865.8
New England	1659.3	17.7	1954.8	14.3	2234.8	22.1	2728.1	14.9	3135.3
United States	9638.1	33.5	12,866.0	32.7	17,069.5	35.9	23,191.9	35.6	31,443.3

Source: U. S. Census Office. Eighth Census (1860), *Preliminary Report on the Eighth Census. 1860.* (Washington: Government Printing Office, 1862), 127-31.

Table III-5. Proportions of New England States' Population Living in Towns of 0-2499, 2500-9999, and over 10,000, 1830-1860

State or Area	*0-2499*	*2500-9999*	*10,000 and over*	*0-2499*	*2500-9999*	*10,000 and over*	*0-2499*	*2500-9999*	*10,000 and over*	*0-2499*	*2500-9999*	*10,000 and over*
	1830			*1840*			*1850*			*1860*		
Maine	79.6	17.2	3.2	72.2	24.8	3.0	63.8	30.2	6.0	62.0	31.2	6.8
New Hampshire	86.0	14.0	—	78.6	21.4	—	73.9	21.7	4.4	74.1	16.7	9.2
Vermont	89.3	10.7	—	86.6	13.4	—	78.1	21.9	—	78.3	21.7	—
Northern New England	84.3	14.4	1.3	77.8	20.8	1.4	70.1	25.9	4.0	69.1	25.2	5.7
MASSACHUSETTS	55.7	32.0	12.3	44.5	36.0	19.5	34.1	33.4	32.5	31.2	30.9	37.9
Connecticut	48.2	48.4	3.4	51.2	44.6	4.2	38.7	52.2	9.1	33.3	50.6	17.1
Rhode Island	25.2	54.5	20.3	25.7	53.0	21.3	13.0	51.0	36.0	11.1	39.5	49.4
Southern New England	50.5	39.3	10.2	44.3	39.1	16.6	33.1	42.8	27.1	29.8	36.9	33.3
New England	66.9	27.2	5.9	53.0	37.8	9.2	49.6	33.6	16.8	45.7	32.1	22.2

Sources: U. S. Census Office. Fifth Census (1830), *Fifth Census; or, Enumeration of the Inhabitants of the United States, as Corrected at the Department of State. 1830. . . .* (Washington: Duff Green, 1832), 3-9, 11-13, 31-35, 17-21, 27-29, 25; U. S. Census Office. Sixth Census (1840), *Sixth Census or Enumeration of the Inhabitants of the United States, as Corrected at the Department of State, in 1840. . . .* (Washington: Blair & Rives, 1841), 5-19, 25-31, 69-75, 37-47, 59-63, 53; U. S. Census Office. Seventh Census (1850), *The Seventh Census of the United States: 1850. . . .* (Washington: Robert Armstrong, 1853), 4-7, 20-21, 34-36, 50-52, 78-79, 67; U. S. Census Office. Eighth Census, *Population of the United States in 1860,* 200-206, 306-309, 494-497, 220-226, 38-40, 444.

Table III-6. Rate of Change, 1850-1860, in Population Born in New England States and Living There, *versus* Population Born in New England but Living Outside Area or State of Birth

Area or State of Birth	*Born in Area or State and Still Living There (% Change)*	*Born in Area or State but Living Outside It (% Change)*
Maine	15.6	72.8
New Hampshire	3.0	14.3
Vermont	9.6	20.0
Northern New England	10.5	35.6
MASSACHUSETTS	16.4	17.9
Connecticut	6.5	– 1.5[a]
Rhode Island	6.5	4.6
Southern New England	12.5	8.4
New England	11.5	23.8

[a] The negative rate indicates that deaths of Connecticut natives residing outside Connecticut were exceeding out-migration from Connecticut to other states.

Sources: U. S. Census Office. Seventh Census (1850), *The Seventh Census of the United States: 1850,* xxxvi; U. S. Census Office. Eighth Census (1860), *Population of the United States in 1860,* 616-19.

foreign-born (see Tables III-6, III-7, and III-8, respectively). In each of three categories, northern New England's performance lagged markedly behind the growth or change rates of southern New England, suggesting that the northern areas were less attractive to the three groups (natives, in-migrants, and immigrants) than were the southern. Slower over-all northern population growth rates also accompanied slower growth rates for places of over 2500 population.

Massachusetts, more than Connecticut or Rhode Island, benefited from these trends: it acted as a collecting basin for in-migrants from the other five New England states. Table III-9 shows the proportions of out-migrants from the other New England states who chose to settle in Massachusetts. During the 1850's, persons leaving northern New England tended ever more to move to areas other than Massachusetts, while Massachusetts became more pop-

Table III-7. Net Per Cent Change, 1850-1860, in Native-Born Population Born Outside New England States but Living in Them

	Per Cent Change, 1850-1860	
Area or State of Residence	*Native-Born Population Born Outside Area or State But Living in It*	*Total Population*
Maine	–12.6[a]	7.7
New Hampshire	7.0	2.6
Vermont	–15.2[a]	0.3
Northern New England	–6.9[a]	4.5
MASSACHUSETTS	17.5	23.8
Connecticut	40.9	42.1
Rhode Island	28.0	18.4
Southern New England	23.2	23.5
New England	11.0	14.9
United States	38.3	35.6

[a] A negative rate indicates that in-migration of natives of another state or area was falling behind deaths and out-migration of such persons.

Sources: U. S. Census Office. Seventh Census (1850), *The Seventh Census of the United States: 1850,* xxxvi; U. S. Census Office. Eighth Census (1860), *Population of the United States in 1860,* 616-19; Table III-4.

ular as a goal for out-migrants from Connecticut (very slightly) and Rhode Island.

Massachusetts likewise became a magnet for foreigners, attracting a majority of New England's foreign-born by 1850, and increasing its lead during the 'fifties (see Table III-10).

Within Massachusetts, Boston was the home of substantial numbers of in-migrants and immigrants, but from 1850 to 1860, the city never contained a majority of any of Massachusetts' in-migrant or immigrant groups. In fact, the city's share of the state's immigrants fell after 1850, from 29.0 per cent in 1850 to 25.4 per cent in 1855 and 24.5 per cent in 1860.[10] Similar declines occurred for all immigrant groups and for most in-migrant groups except those from Vermont, Connecticut, and Rhode Island (see Table

Table III-8. Net Per Cent Changes, 1850-1860, in Numbers of Foreign-Born Residing in New England and the United States

	Per Cent Change, 1850-1860, by Area or State of Residence				
Country or Area of Birth	*Northern New England*	*Massa-chusetts*	*Southern New England*	*New England*	*United States*
Ireland	9.1	60.0	68.0	56.5	67.7
England and Wales	39.3	43.1	49.0	47.4	55.0
Germany	55.1	130.6	210.3	195.5	127.0
Scotland	26.1	53.5	48.0	43.3	53.9
Canada (modern area)	21.3	70.7	85.2	44.6	69.2
Other Foreign	36.0	92.6	87.5	79.8	160.1
Total Foreign	17.0	61.6	70.9	56.9	87.1
Total Population	4.5	23.8	23.5	14.9	35.6

Sources: U. S. Census Office. Seventh Census (1850), *The Seventh Census of the United States: 1850,* xxxvii; U. S. Census Office. Eighth Census (1860), *Population of the United States in 1860,* 620-23; Table III-4.

III-11). Boston had proportionately more persons from Maine, New Hampshire, and all major foreign countries, as compared with the city's share of state population, than did the rest of the state. Conversely, it housed smaller proportions of persons born in Massachusetts, Vermont, Connecticut, and Rhode Island than did the rest of Massachusetts, assuming as a norm equal state-wide population distribution of all groups. During the 'fifties Boston gained in-migrants from these four states faster than did the rest of the state, while outstate Massachusetts attracted foreign immigrants to a greater extent than Boston did.

Until well after 1860, the majority of northern New Englanders lived in towns of under 2500 population, while southern New England achieved a majority in towns of over 2500 population shortly before 1850. As one might guess, in-migrants to Boston from the rest of New England did not strictly reflect the division of the region's population into rural and urban (using the 2500-

Table III-9. Proportions, by Per Cent, of Out-Migrants from Other New England States Residing in Massachusetts, 1850 and 1860, and Net Change, 1850-1860, of Their Number

Area or State of Birth	*Per Cent of Out-Migrants From That Area Living in Massachusetts*		*Net Per Cent Change, 1850-1860, in Number of Out-Migrants From That Area Living in Massachusetts*
	1850	*1860*	
Maine	43.9	34.8	46.0
New Hampshire	36.1	35.1	11.3
Vermont	12.1	10.7	5.6
Northern New England	32.6	29.3	21.9
Connecticut	10.1	10.2	−0.1[a]
Rhode Island	26.4	29.4	16.7
Connecticut plus Rhode Island	4.6	4.6	7.0
New England without Massachusetts	21.8	21.9	18.4

[a] The negative rate indicates that deaths of Connecticut natives in, and out-migration of Connecticut natives from, Massachusetts together surpassed the inflow to Massachusetts of Connecticut natives.

Sources: U. S. Census Office. Seventh Census (1850), *The Seventh Census of the United States: 1850,* xxxvi; U. S. Census Office. Eighth Census (1860), *Population of the United States in 1860,* 616-19.

person criterion) segments. Inquiring into the question of which size community sample members presumably grew up in gives results shown in Table III–12. By 1860, when 54.3 per cent of all New Englanders resided in places of over 2500 population, only 33.7 per cent of the New-England-born (outside Boston) sample members had grown up in such places. Even allowing for the 20-year lag built in to the figures, this indicates the pronounced rural origins of Boston's in-migrants. But it is doubtful that most New-England-born sample members still resided in the towns of their birth as late as their twentieth year. Of all New-England-born members of the 1860 sample who were not residing in Boston

Table III-10. Proportion of New England's Foreign-Born Residing in Massachusetts, 1850 and 1860, and Net Per Cent Change, 1850-1860, of Their Number

Country or Area of Birth	*Per Cent of New England's Residents From That Area Living in Massachusetts*		*Per Cent Gain in Number of Residents From That Area and Living in Massachusetts, 1850-1860*
	1850	*1860*	
Ireland	58.9	60.2	60.0
England and Wales	53.3	51.7	43.1
Germany	62.8	49.0	130.6
Scotland	47.5	50.8	53.5
Canada (modern area)	32.4	38.1	70.7
Other Foreign	59.9	64.2	92.6
Total Foreign	53.8	55.4	61.6

Sources: U. S. Census Office. Seventh Census (1850), *The Seventh Census of the United States: 1850,* xxxvii; U. S. Census Office. Eighth Census (1860), *Population of the United States in 1860,* 620-23.

in 1850, only one was located in the manuscript census of his birthplace town in 1850—and that individual was then only 16 years old. This would seem to indicate not only leaving one's hometown at a precocious age but also an erratic progression or "stage migration" thence to Boston, with at least one intermediate residence. Parenthetically, this next residence after the birthplace town would appear—at least for our 1860 sample members—not to have been another major city, principal manufacturing center, or major railroad junction in Massachusetts, for the manuscript censuses of 1850 for such areas disclosed none of the missing 1860 sample members. Perhaps individuals worked their way to Boston from one village or farm to another.*

* A sequel to this study will attempt, among other efforts, to elucidate the migration processes. See also Joseph F. Kett, "Growing Up in Rural New England, 1800–1840," in Tamara K. Hareven (ed.), *Anonymous Americans: Explorations in Nineteenth-Century Social History* (Englewood Cliffs, N. J.: Prentice-Hall, 1971), 1–16.

Table III-11. Boston's Share of Massachusetts' Population, by Birthplace, 1850 and 1860, and Net Per Cent Change in Number of Such Persons, 1850-1860

Area or Place of Birth	*Boston's Per Cent of Persons Living in Massachusetts and Born in a Given Area*		*Net Per Cent Change, 1850-1860, in Number of Persons Living in Boston and in Outstate Massachusetts and Born in a Given Area*	
	1850	*1860*	*Boston*	*Outstate Massachusetts*
Maine	26.0	25.8	44.6	46.5
New Hampshire	16.8	16.1	6.6	12.2
Vermont	9.9	12.2	30.4	2.9
MASSACHUSETTS	9.9	10.7	26.0	14.8
Connecticut	3.7	4.8	30.1	–0.1[a]
Rhode Island	5.1	5.4	23.2	16.5
Total United States Outside Massachusetts	15.5	16.6	35.5	22.7
Ireland	30.4	24.8	30.5	72.8
England and Wales	19.0	17.1	28.7	46.5
Germany	41.2	32.2	80.4	165.9
Scotland	20.1	19.3	47.3	55.0
Canada (modern area)	} 33.2	25.2	} 43.0	} 90.3
Other Foreign		35.2		
Total Foreign	29.0	24.5	36.7	72.0

[a] The negative rate indicates that in-migration of Connecticut natives to outstate Massachusetts did not keep pace with the total of Connecticut natives' out-migration from, and deaths in, outstate Massachusetts.

Sources: U. S. Census Office. Seventh Census (1850), *Statistical View of the United States,* 399; U. S. Census Office. Seventh Census (1850), *The Seventh Census of the United States: 1850,* xxxvi, xxxvii; U. S. Census Office. Eighth Census (1860), *Population of the United States in 1860,* 608, 616-23.

Table III-12. Size of Birthplace of Sample Members at Their Age 20, for Sample Members from Outstate Massachusetts, from the Other New England States, and from all New England (outside Boston), 1830-1860, by Per Cent

	Area of Birth		
Town Size	*Outstate Massachusetts*	*Other Five New England States*	*New England Outside Boston*
1830 Sample			
0-999	16.1	28.6	19.0
1000-2499	48.4	42.9	47.1
2500-9999	33.3	28.6	32.3
10,000 and over	2.2	–	1.7
Number of sample members	93	28	121
1840 Sample			
0-999	10.5	12.8	11.1
1000-2499	54.3	61.5	56.2
2500-9999	31.4	25.6	29.9
10,000 and over	3.8	–	2.7
Number of sample members	105	39	144
1850 Sample			
0-999	11.8	9.6	10.8
1000-2499	48.5	65.4	55.8
2500-9999	38.2	19.2	30.0
10,000 and over	1.5	5.8	3.3
Number of sample members	68	52	120
1860 Sample			
0-999	12.8	8.5	10.2
1000-2499	51.3	59.3	56.1
2500-9999	28.2	23.7	25.5
10,000 and over	7.7	8.5	8.2
Number of sample members	39	59	98

Source: Sample data.

Boston thus shared in some population changes more than in others. Northern New Englanders were leaving their area so rapidly that state growth rates were considerably depressed after 1840. Disproportionately large numbers of persons from Maine and New Hampshire found their way to Boston, while the opposite held for Vermonters (who tended to move to New York and westward). These out-migrants did participate in a population concentration process, but outside their area of birth. Persons born in outstate Massachusetts tended to move to larger places during 1830–60, but more and more these persons chose to live outside Boston, often in its suburbs (*cf.* Table II-4). People from Connecticut and Rhode Island chose overwhelmingly, in moving to Massachusetts, to live outside Boston; but many more of them removed to New York than to Massachusetts.[11] Generally, New England in-migrants to Boston tended, about two to one, to have been born and to have grown up in places of under 2500 population. This proportion did not vary too much during the antebellum period.

Foreigners who moved to New England preferred to live in Massachusetts, probably because so many of them arrived at the port of Boston. While Boston had more foreigners, in proportion to its fraction of the state's population, than did the rest of Massachusetts, it never had a state-wide majority of any foreign group. After 1850, foreigners participated in the slight general trend of higher growth rates of eastern Massachusetts towns outside Boston. By 1860, the city's proportion of native-born (by place of birth) was rising again, but because of native births to foreign-born parents. The city which had been approximately 95 per cent native-born in 1830 probably had about 40–45 per cent native-born of native parents by 1860.

IV

Population Mobility and Redistribution in Boston, 1830–1860

> The character of the population among whom I minister is very fluctuating. In fact, it is the characteristic of the poor everywhere, to be continually shifting their places of abode. The Missionary's word just begins to find a lodgement when the door abruptly closes; the chain of communion is broken, with but little probability of ever being united again.
>
> REV. SAMUEL B. CRUFT[1]

Three guides stand ready to conduct us through a maze of relationships, quantities, and assumptions to our goal: a greater understanding of some of the processes of population mobility and redistribution, particularly with respect to Boston's native- and foreign-born ante-bellum inhabitants. The three guides are censuses, city directories, and the 1540-member sample of household heads which is the keel of this study. Like many guides, however, these three are of dissimilar prowess. In some areas their capabilities overlap, complementing each other, while in others they are absent or unreliable. No one guide leads us through the entire labyrinth.

The censuses and city directories both date from the ante-bellum era, but since city directories provide more advanced insights into population mobility than do censuses, and since censuses have traditionally guided questers through the early turnings of the maze, let us follow censuses as far as they can lead. Thence we may push forward, led by city directories and the study sample.

Censuses of Boston for 1830, 1845, 1850, 1855, and 1865 gathered data which may be coaxed to demonstrate what was happening in the gradual net redistribution of native- and foreign-born groups during the ante-bellum era (see Table IV-1). In 1830, foreign-born were much over-represented proportionately in the central area of Boston, and under-represented in outlying areas of the city. Their numbers were only about twice those of the Negro community, and certainly the foreign-born were much the less "visible." But during the fifteen years following 1830, Boston experienced unprecedented growth: its population almost doubled, while the "foreign element" increased sevenfold. In 1845, more than 110,000 persons called the city their home. Considerable seepage of foreign-born into Boston's central area had occurred by 1845. By 1850, there was striking agreement in distribution of foreign-born and that of the total population. A decade and a half later, after the Civil War, the foreign-born seem to have been drifting inward once more.

Looking at the situation from the viewpoint of households and not individuals may be instructive. If the earliest censuses had been more detailed, they would have produced data like those in Table IV-2, which, although based on the study sample, is appropriate here. The table differentiates some of Boston's major population components, showing their distribution in core and periphery by proportion of households, not individuals. According to this source, the foreign-born were still disproportionately concentrated in the core in 1840. Considering both the census and sample information, we note that the foreign-born remained over-concentrated in central Boston until sometime between 1845 and 1850, when they presumably decentralized in large numbers, achieving by 1850 a core/periphery distribution almost identical to that of the whole population. Other measures of mobility corroborate this foreign Diaspora of the late 'forties. Native-born individuals and households, on the other hand, consistently remained slightly more peripherally distributed than did the total population, with no large-scale shifts apparent. To glean further information on movements of population components, we must abandon

Table IV-1. Central and Peripheral Shares of Boston's Alien, Foreign-Born, and Native-Born Population, 1830, 1845, 1850, 1855, 1865

Area	*Total Population*	*Aliens*	*Aliens as Per Cent of Total*	*Native-Born and Naturalized*	*Native-Born and Naturalized as Per Cent of Total*
1830					
Center	25,416	1,907	7.5	23,509	92.5
Periphery	35,976	1,561	4.3	34,415	95.7
Center Per Cent	41.4	55.0		40.5	
Periphery Per Cent	58.6	45.0		59.5	
		Foreign-Born	*Foreign-Born as Per Cent of Total*	*Native-Born*	*Native-Born as Per Cent of Total*
1845					
Center	57,481	14,578	25.4	42,903	74.6
Periphery	56,885	12,526	22.0	44,359	78.0
Center Per Cent	50.3	53.8		49.1	
Periphery Per Cent	49.7	46.2		50.9	
1850 (Old Wards, State Census)					
Center	60,647	27,812	45.9	32,835	54.1
Periphery	78,141	35,654	45.6	42,487	54.4
Center Per Cent	43.7	43.8		43.6	
Periphery Per Cent	56.3	56.2		56.4	

1850 (New Wards, State Census)					
Center	74,289	34,407	46.3	39,882	53.7
Periphery	64,499	29,059	45.1	35,440	54.9
Center Per Cent	53.5	54.2		52.9	
Periphery Per Cent	46.5	45.8		47.1	
1855					
Center	80,806	43,407	53.7	37,399	46.3
Periphery	80,623	42,100	52.2	38,523	47.8
Center Per Cent	50.1	50.8		47.2	
Periphery Per Cent	49.9	49.2		52.8	
1865					
Center	75,688	28,718	37.9[a]	46,970	62.1[a]
Periphery	116,630	37,103	31.8[a]	79,527	68.2[a]
Center Per Cent	39.4	43.7		37.2	
Periphery Per Cent	60.6	56.3		62.8	

[a]In and before 1855, "aliens" included the *children* of foreign-born, regardless of birthplace of the children.

Sources: U.S. Census Office. Fifth Census (1830), *Fifth Census; or, Enumeration of the Inhabitants of the United States, as Corrected at the Department of State. 1830. . . .* (Washington: Duff Green, 1832), 20-21; Lemuel Shattuck, *Report to the Committee of the City Council Appointed to Obtain the Census of Boston for the Year 1845, ...* (Boston: John H. Eastburn, 1846), Appendix 20; *Boston City Document No. 42* (1850), 30; *Report of the Joint Special Committee on the Census of Boston, May, 1855, ...* (Boston: Moore & Crosby, 1856), 7; Massachusetts. Secretary of the Commonwealth, *Abstract of the Census of Massachusetts, 1865: With Remarks. . . .* (Boston: Wright & Potter, 1867), 76; total city figures, but not ward-by-ward figures, are available for 1860 in U.S. Census Office. Eighth Census (1860), *Population of the United States in 1860; . . . .* (Washington: Government Printing Office, 1864), 608.

Table IV-2. Core and Peripheral Residence of Various Components of the Study Sample, Compared with Census Results, 1830, 1840, 1850, and 1860 (by Per Cent)

	Area of Birth					
	Massachusetts	*United States*	*Ireland*	*Foreign*	*Total Sample*	*Households (census)*
1830						
Core	35.0	33.6	62.9	61.9	37.7	37.3
Periphery	65.0	66.4	37.1	38.1	62.3	62.7
N	100	128	35	42	385	9,518
1840						
Core	54.2	53.2	66.0	61.8	57.6	58.3
Periphery	45.8	46.8	34.0	38.2	42.4	41.7
N	142	188	50	68	385	14,047
1850						
Core	40.7	43.1	41.7	39.8	41.6	41.3
Periphery	59.3	56.9	58.3	60.2	58.4	58.7
N	125	202	144	181	385	24,667
1860						
Core	44.3	43.5	46.6	42.3	42.6	42.6
Periphery	55.7	56.5	53.4	57.7	57.4	57.4
N	88	170	161	215	385	33,633

Sources: Sample data; count of households in manuscript federal censuses of Boston, 1830, 1840, 1850, and 1860 (microfilm from National Archives).

census data and venture on with the help of city directories and of the study sample.

Between 1830 and 1857 the compilers of Boston's city directories claimed to have included a total of 596,124 names in their volumes (this total took in many duplications, of course; the term "separate listings" would have been more appropriate). During those years, changes in the locations of persons and firms listed in the directories necessitated some 509,866 changes in the directories, equal to 85.5 per cent of the total number of listings.[2] In yearly tables, the directory compilers rendered an account of population movements under the rubrics "names dropped" (which included deaths), "names added" (which included those reaching age 21), "removals, &c.," and "total alterations." "Total alterations" is now known more elegantly (in its reference to persons and not firms) as "residential mobility." The principal present concern is to examine this mobility, as it related to native or foreign birth and some ancillary characteristics, in ante-bellum Boston.

The reader may wish to think of population movements in a delimited area, such as that of pre-Civil-War Boston, in terms of some of the activities of a modern bank clearing-house. Such clearing-houses strike daily credits and debits, and then by the transfer of relatively small amounts of money even up the accounts of participating member banks. In some ways, Boston acted as a "people clearing-house." In-migration (and births) accrued credits, out-migration (and deaths) incurred debits, and censuses at five-year intervals provided new balance sheets showing how people were distributed among the sections or wards of the city, here analogous to the member banks of the clearing-house association.

But looking at balance sheets, or censuses, has carried us only so far, for such information is but a static representation, a "snapshot," of a dynamic phenomenon. Just as examining clearing-house account balances at day's end does not reveal the intensity or turnover of that day's transactions, so do censuses fail to disclose ongoing population movements. The census gives the results of a period's transactions, in terms of net loss or net gain of the city's sub-areas. We are interested, on the other hand, in the transactions producing the result—in short, in watching the "central clearing-house's" vital "funds" flow from one to another "bank."

This chapter examines several aspects of residential mobility, using both city directory data and information from a detailed tracing of the residential movements, 1830–59, of the 1540 heads of household in the study sample. Four major general conclusions emerge from this dual examination. First, population turnover within Boston was much greater than censuses would lead us to believe, because each population stream had a counter-stream, and large total movements produced small net population changes. Second, mobility varied over the thirty ante-bellum years, remaining relatively level until the mid-1840's, then rising sharply to a new plateau. Third, just as some banks are busier than others some days, so various components of the population were differentially mobile at times. There seems to have been a strong relationship between native or foreign birth and mobility in respect to both duration of residence and to change of residence. Native-born persons passing through Boston during part of their lives (for most sample members Boston was a way station on their trip through life) stayed in the city, on an average, two to three times as long during the 1830–60 period as did foreign-born persons. Probably this was due to the foreigners' generally later arrival times during the period. Once they were settled in the city, foreign-born individuals moved around much more than did native-born Americans. Fourth, Boston's net population growth was the resultant of several population vectors. It is possible, through the sample, to gain an approximate notion of those vectors' magnitude and direction.

The principal aid in this entire undertaking is of course the city directory, which attempted yearly to locate and list the city's resident heads of household. It would be only too easy to reproduce the tables printed annually by the directories to show "alterations," then point to these tables as quantifying residential mobility. This would be possible had the city directories been perfect, but they were man-made, hence were not all-knowing, and thus not all-telling.[3] Here the guiding assumption has been that errors and omissions in the directories were equally distributed between "names added" and "names dropped," i.e., that the compilers were as likely to miss adding a name as to drop one. This was probably not so, but it would be extremely difficult to determine the "actual" error differential. By taking the "names added" (or in-migration plus local residents reaching the age of 21) and "names dropped" (or out-migration plus deaths of household heads) as about equally inaccurate, we may nonetheless use their *ratio* to help gauge population turnover.

By dealing in the present case only with adults, heads of household, we by-pass the knotty problem of determining "net natural increase" (the excess of births over deaths), for the units of the study become adults, whose attainment of age 21 or whose dying were much more likely to have been recorded than were the births and deaths (often concomitant) of multitudes of children in a city where average age at death was about 22 years.[4] From age profiles of the population one may make crude estimates for each decade of the number of individuals reaching age 21; fragmentary death records provide data for an approximation of the number of deaths of individuals aged 20 and over (the assumptions being that all such males, and one-sixth of such females, were household heads). These estimates appear in Table IV-3. A comparison of the number of city directory listings with the number of households in the city reveals that there were ordinarily between 1.25 and 1.40 directory listings per household. The "surplus" listings were presumably accounted for by business

Table IV-3. Estimated Numbers of Males Reaching Age 21, and of Deaths of Household Heads (Aged 20 and over), By Decade, Boston, 1830-1860

		Decade	
Group	*1830-1840*	*1840-1850*	*1850-1860*
Estimated number of males reaching age 21[a]	8,250	10,500	13,500
Estimated number of deaths of household heads[b]	4,600	6,350	10,246

[a]Estimated by taking ten times the difference (number of males aged 20 at end of decade)—(number of males aged 20 at start of decade).

[b]Estimated by taking the total number of deaths of males aged 21 and over, plus one-sixth the total number of deaths of females aged 21 and over (to allow for female heads of household).

Sources: Shattuck, *Report to the Committee of the City Council,* Appendix 14, Appendix 15, Appendix 17-Appendix 19; Massachusetts. Secretary of the Commonwealth, *Abstract of the Census of the Commonwealth of Massachusetts... June, 1855...* (Boston: William White, 1857), 89-90; Massachusetts. Secretary of the Commonwealth, *Abstract of the Census of Massachusetts, 1860, from the Eighth U.S. Census, with Remarks on the Same...* (Boston: Wright & Potter, 1863), 46-49; Lemuel Shattuck, *The Vital Statistics of Boston;... for the Last Twenty-Nine Years...* (Philadelphia: Lea & Blanchard, 1841), 13; *Boston City Documents Nos. 4* (1850), 20; *10* (1851), 19, 24; *7* (1852), 13; *10* (1853), 12; *12* (1854), 16; *10* (1855), 22; *10* (1856), 30; *14* (1857), 27; *9* (1858), 24; *13* (1859), 29-40; *85* (1860), 44-45.

firms, second listings for households having sons over 21, and persons living in hotels and boarding-houses (which counted as single households). Dividing the directories' "names added" and "names dropped" figures by the appropriate ratios, and calling the results "households added" and "households dropped," we obtain the figures in Table IV-4. Then, subtracting from "households

Table IV-4. Estimates of "Households Added" and "Households Dropped" in Boston City Directories, 1830-1860

Group	Decade 1830-40	1840-50	1850-60
Initial number of households (census)	9,518	14,047	24,667
Estimated "households added"	+26,575	+38,400	+63,900
Estimated "households dropped"	-22,050	-27,800	-55,000
Surplus of "households added"	(+ 4,525)	(+10,600)	(+ 8,900)
Estimated final number of households	14,043	24,647	33,567
Actual final number of households (census)	14,047	24,667	33,633

Sources: Number of households from manuscript federal censuses of Boston, 1830, 1840, 1850, and 1860 (microfilm from National Archives); estimates from data in Boston city directories, 1831-57, as explained in accompanying text.

added" the estimated number of males reaching age 21 in each decade, and subtracting from "households dropped" the estimated number of deaths of household heads, as given in Table IV-3, there remains the estimated in- and out-migration shown in Table IV-5. It is plain that at least twice as many households passed through in each of the three decades as lived in the city at the start of any of the decades.

These figures show the vast increase in the importance of migration as a factor in Boston's population growth. During the 'thirties, net in-migration (or the "surplus of in-migration") accounted for about one-fifth the net increase in the city's households, while four-fifths came from local residents who attained the age of 21. By the 'forties, net in-migration supplied about

Table IV-5. Estimated In- and Out-Migration of Households, Boston, 1830-1860

Migration Group (households)	*Decade*		
	1830-40	*1840-50*	*1850-60*
Estimated in-migration	18,325	27,900	50,400
Estimated out-migration	17,450	21,450	44,754
Surplus of in-migration	(875)	(6,450)	(5,646)

Sources: Derived from Tables IV-3 and IV-4 as explained in accompanying text.

three-fifths of the city's net gain in households; and in the 'fifties that proportion advanced slightly, to about two-thirds. These indicated population turnover rates may seem incredible. Certainly census data, which show net, rather than aggregate, changes, do not suggest such findings.

Other evidence corroborates these high turnover rates among Boston's ante-bellum residents. Table IV-6 shows, for selected years, the persistence in Boston of sample members. (Since determining whether a sample member was "present" was sometimes difficult, there may be discrepancies between some of these figures and those presented in the next chapter. The present fig-

Table IV-6. Per Cent of Sample Members Present in Boston at Start of Selected Years, 1830-1860 (N = 385 in Each Sample)

Year	*Per Cent Present in Sample of*			
	1830	*1840*	*1850*	*1860*
1830	100.0	40.8	20.5	11.4
1831	84.4	42.4	20.8	12.0
1835	63.2	56.4	24.9	15.1
1839	49.1	80.8	30.4	17.7
1840	43.9	100.0	32.7	18.5
1841	42.4	89.6	35.1	19.2
1845	34.0	68.3	46.2	24.7
1849	27.8	50.9	72.4	33.5
1850	25.7	48.6	100.0	38.4
1851	24.4	44.4	88.0	39.7
1855	17.2	33.0	61.0	52.7
1859	13.3	27.8	42.1	77.1
1860	12.2	27.6	39.0	100.0

Source: Sample data.

ures suffice as an example, however.) Between 1830 and 1831, 15.6 per cent of the 1830 sample left Boston. The corresponding figures for the 1840 and 1850 samples, in 1840–41 and 1850–51 respectively, were 10.4 per cent and 12.0 per cent. Again, between 1839 and 1840, 19.2 per cent of the 1840 sample arrived in Boston. The corresponding percentages for the 1850 sample in 1849–50 and for the 1860 sample in 1859–60 were, respectively, 27.6 and 22.9. These figures suggest an annual turnover *c.* 1830 and 1840 of about 30 per cent, increasing to about 40 per cent *c.* 1850 and 1860. Taking as an example a group of 1000 persons who live in an area, imagine that 30 per cent of the group leaves yearly, with no replacement. At the end of ten years, only 28 persons will remain. Yet, if we analogize the 1000-member group to a city, replacement enters the picture. Over a ten-year period in the "city" of 1000 persons, not only has the departure of 972 persons not reduced the population, net in-migration and net natural increase have raised the total population above the original 1000 mark. Thus, for the original group there has been a turnover of at least 1,944 (= 2 × 972) persons. Extending the analogy yet further, we might represent the population each year by the 1000 figure, reducing it yearly by 30 per cent and simultaneously increasing it by slightly more than 30 per cent. Many such series would operate all at once, and total turnover for a decade could easily reach several times the initial 1000.

An alternate approach is to derive from Table IV-6 the percentage rates of growth or decay for the sample groups (see Table IV-7). These samples show their highest rates of change in the years just before and just after the samples' census years, gradually falling off until the rate of gain or loss stabilizes at about 7 or 8 per cent per year 20 years on either "side" of the samples' census years. It is worth noting that with an annual growth or decay rate of 7 per cent, half of a population will enter or leave a city in 9.6 years. But if the rate is raised to 8 per cent, the time decreases to 8.3 years; if to 10 per cent, then 6.6 years; 15 per cent, 4.3 years; 20 per cent, 3.1 years; 30 per cent, 1.94 years; and 40 per cent, 1.36 years. Assuming that the turnover rates in the years on either "side" of the census years were in fact typical of the entire ante-

Table IV-7. Annual Growth or Decay Rates of the Samples (Per Cent)

Decay: Number of Years After Sample Year	*Sample Groups and Rates (Per Cent)*			
	1830	*1840*	*1850*	*1860*
1	15.60	10.40	12.00	n.a.[a]
5	10.84	9.09	11.62	n.a.
10	8.74	7.70	9.93	n.a.
20	6.90	6.55	n.a.	n.a.
30	7.00	n.a.	n.a.	n.a.
Growth: Number of Years Before Sample Year				
1	n.a.[a]	19.20	27.60	22.90
5	n.a.	13.34	17.56	14.80
10	n.a.	9.48	11.68	10.09
20	n.a.	n.a.	8.00	8.50
30	n.a.	n.a.	n.a.	7.21

[a] n.a. = not available. Since the study gathered no data outside the thirty years of its concern, it is not possible to calculate growth or decay of the samples outside those limits.

Source: Calculated from data in Table IV-6, using the formulae G/DR = 100% x (1-r) and

$$r = \frac{1}{p^{(n-1)}},$$

where *G/DR* represents the growth or decay rate in per cent, *p* represents the proportion of persons (a figure between 0 and 1) present in Boston after *n* years, and *r* stands for the annual ratio of growth or decay (analogous to *r* in geometric series).

bellum period, the rates for the whole era would have averaged about 30 to 40 per cent, implying that one-half of Boston's population would disappear and be replaced every one or two years. Thus, this method indicates that total decadal turnover could reach several times the city's total population. It is important to stress this point since census returns, which report only net population changes, completely neglect the matter of turnover.*

* To calculate these "half-life" periods, use $\frac{\log 2}{\text{colog } r} = n$ years, where r and n are defined as in Table IV-7.

It would seem, then, that over-all mobility in ante-bellum Boston was at least as large as the oft-quoted modern figures for the United States: 20 per cent per year, or "one family in five moves every year." The actual turnover rate for ante-bellum Boston was higher yet. Having established the plausibility of an annual rate of at least 30 per cent, let us proceed to examine that mobility, particularizing portions of it. Generally speaking, mobility varied during 1830–60, remaining nearly level until the mid-1840's, then finding a newer, higher level. The city directories' "total alterations" classification provides a sensitive measure of this phenomenon, for the proportion of "total alterations" to total listings rose sharply after 1842, reaching a figure of over 90 per cent by 1845 (see Table IV-8).

Table IV-8. "Total Alterations"[a] as Per Cent of Total Listings in Boston City Directories, 1831-1856[b]

Period	*Total Listings*	*"Total Alterations"*[a]	*"Total Alterations" as Per Cent of Total Listings*
1831-34	51,658	37,169	72.0
1835-39	77,737	59,542	76.6
1840-44	100,225	76,064	75.9
1845, 1848-49[b]	87,988	83,310	94.7
1850-54	189,792	172,466	90.9
1855-56[b]	88,724	81,325	91.7

[a] "Total alterations" is the sum of "names added," "names dropped," and "removals, &c."

[b] No figures are available for the years 1830, 1846 (Adams' directory), 1847, 1857, 1858, 1859, and 1860.

Source: Boston city directories, 1831-56, with exceptions as in [b].

The samples also provide residential mobility measurements, but they suffer from a drawback in that they are longitudinal rather than cross-sectional like the directories. That is, knowing about the mobility (say) in 1831 of the 1830 sample members reveals little about total mobility in Boston during 1831, for by 1831 the 1830 sample was "losing touch," or representativeness, with the population. To gauge the 1831 situation would require an 1831 sample, which is impossible since no 1831 census was taken. But if the samples nearest in time to the year for which we desire information both agree generally on the trend of activity for that year, it would seem safe to assume their indications to be not too far from the "real" situation. This is about as near as we can approach the problem in the absence of yearly censuses and samples.

How, then, to measure residential mobility? Clearly any such measure must derive the rate of change of residence per unit time. Changes of residence appear from a comparison, for each sample member, of his addresses in consecutive city directories. But how can one compute averages for a group whose members stay in Boston for varying periods? A solution is to denominate one year's residence in Boston by a sample member as one "residence-year," a measure analogous to man-hours. One then computes the ratio $\frac{\text{total moves}}{\text{total residence-years}}$ to obtain an expression of residential mobility for a group. For analysis of population mobility and redistribution, the 1830–59 period was divided into six inclusive quinquennia, 1830–34, 1835–39, 1840–44, etc. Table IV-9 shows how, as each sample group approached its census year, it achieved its maximum residential mobility. The values for the census years were 0.358 in 1830, 0.307 in 1840, 0.338 in 1850, and 0.496 in 1860. (Averages for the census years may be lower than those for the circumjacent quinquennium because the number of sample members fell off sharply on either "side" of the census years, reducing the base from which ratios were calculated, and possibly inflating the ratios.)

In practice, these ratios mean that about one household in three moved during each of the four sample years, and presumably in the non-sample years as well, assuming the sample years typical of their times. Even this ratio, nearly twice that of today, is an underestimate, for since city directories appeared annually, an individual could be credited with at most one move in any given year. Then too, the directories discriminated against the lowest economic orders, who were among the most mobile

Table IV-9. Mobility Ratios (Total Moves/Residence-Years) for the Sample Groups, 1830-1859

	Sample Group			
Period	*1830*	*1840*	*1850*	*1860*
1830-34	<u>0.342</u>	0.275	0.156	0.147
1835-39	0.266	<u>0.377</u>	0.259	0.188
1840-44	0.229	0.306	0.278	0.240
1845-49	0.213	0.288	<u>0.464</u>	0.355
1850-54	0.209	0.241	0.321	0.285
1855-59	0.205	0.175	0.349	<u>0.417</u>

Source: Sample data. Maxima are underlined.

of the population (Appendix A discusses the degree of the directories' inclusiveness). There is indirect evidence, from a few duplicated directory listings, and from dual appearances in the manuscript census, that some persons, particularly those of lowest socioeconomic status, moved several times yearly. All in all, then, the "true" over-all mobility ratio for the ante-bellum era was probably over 0.4 and perhaps as high as 0.5 when we take into account the large transient or "floating" population, the instability of the lowest socioeconomic groups, and the lack of their inclusion in the city directories. A rule of thumb would be that ante-bellum Bostonians were twice as mobile as mid-twentieth-century Americans.

Without forcing the longitudinal sample measures of mobility into a situation they were not designed to grapple with, we may nevertheless note that the 1850 sample group, during 1845–49, achieved the highest mobility ratio of the ante-bellum era, 0.464. It was just then, in the late 'forties, that mobility, as measured by changes in the city directories, registered a sharp upswing. The samples indicate that mobility dropped slightly during the 'fifties; the city directory changes dipped somewhat then also, but the difference may be insignificant. At least there is substantial agreement.

But, as we shall see, mobility was not evenly distributed throughout all groups in society; neither was persistence. On the whole, the most mobile members of the population were the least persistent, while the least mobile were the most persistent. This was not a necessary situation, for one might imagine a city in which mobility for all groups was high, while persistence varied greatly: for example, a company town whose owners housed all employees, yet did not renew one-year leases on individual dwellings. But in Boston the inverse relationship held; it was marked as between native-born and foreign-born. For example, Table IV-10 shows the persistence, during 1830–60, of various city population components. The disparity between native-born and foreign-born persons narrowed during the period. (Interestingly, preliminary persistence figures for the 1860–70 decade indicate a widening of the gap, with about 53 per cent persistence for native-born, 31 per cent for foreign-born, and 41 per cent for the entire 1860 sample.) The average persistence for all samples rose in the 'thirties, then fell in the 'forties and 'fifties, only to rise again in the 'sixties. Declining persistence tends to corroborate

Table IV-10. Persistence of Residence in Boston During 1830-1860 of Various Sample Components

	1830	*1840*	*1850*
Native-Born			
Total	172	209	202
Living in Boston Ten Years Later	110	138	86
Per Cent	64.0	66.0	42.6
Foreign-Born			
Total	44	68	183
Living in Boston Ten Years Later	18	37	56
Per Cent	40.9	54.4	30.6
Total Sample			
Total	385	385	385
Living in Boston Ten Years Later	163	176	142
Per Cent	42.4[a]	45.7[a]	36.9

[a]The totals for 1830 and 1840 include, respectively, 169 and 108 persons of unknown ethnic background.

Source: Sample data.

the increasing mobility noted earlier: "churning" of the population was on the rise.

If, as has been demonstrated repeatedly, migrants are usually persons in their late teens or early twenties,[5] and if we assume that their average age on arrival in Boston was about 20, we face the intriguing question, after Boston, whither? Aged 30 to 35 or so, where did the out-migrant from Boston go? This cannot occupy us here, but will be treated in Chapter VI.

Foreign-born Bostonians, as well as being less persistent than native-born residents, were more mobile (see Table IV-11). The results in the case of the foreign-born suggest why the 1845–49 period has manifested such high mobility rates; for not only did the 1850 sample then achieve its highest value, but the 1860 sample did too. Census returns show this period as one of considerable net decentralization of Boston's foreign-born residents. Comparing mobility ratios of foreign-born sample members with those of native-born sample members, shown in Table IV-12, demonstrates that mobility ratios for the foreign-born were usually nearly twice as large as those for native-born. Since city directories included proportionately more native-born than foreign-born, the "true" ratio was probably higher than two to one.

To try to grasp some notion of the resultants of all the popula-

Table IV-11. Mobility Ratios (Total Moves/Residence-Years) for Foreign-Born Members of the Sample Groups, 1830-1860

	Sample Group			
Period	*1830*	*1840*	*1850*	*1860*
1830-34	<u>0.414</u>	0.532	0.333	0.529
1835-39	0.285	<u>0.590</u>	0.614	0.512
1840-44	0.264	0.294	0.348	0.450
1845-49	0.326	0.293	<u>0.786</u>	<u>0.567</u>
1850-54	0.207	0.223	0.357	0.363
1855-59	0.250	0.220	0.393	0.561

Source: Sample data. Maxima are underlined.

Table IV-12. Mobility Ratios (Total Moves/Residence-Years) For Native-Born Members of the Sample Groups, 1830-1860

	Sample Group			
Period	*1830*	*1840*	*1850*	*1860*
1830-34	0.274	0.219	0.150	0.118
1835-39	0.207	0.300	0.216	0.142
1840-44	0.176	0.235	0.262	0.187
1845-49	0.167	0.230	0.337	0.287
1850-54	0.193	0.239	0.292	0.245
1855-59	0.192	0.155	0.315	0.296

Source: Sample data. Maxima are underlined.

tion movements going on in ante-bellum Boston, we may examine more minutely the movements of the 1540 sample members into, within, and out of Boston. Having already noted two of the kinds of population movements—in- and out-migration—involved in Boston's ante-bellum growth, there remain six other possible kinds of moves sample members could have made. For the purposes of this study, Boston was divided into core and peripheral areas. Sample members could have moved from outside the city into either core or periphery, could have left the city from the core or the periphery, and could have moved from core to periphery (decentralized) or periphery to core (centralized). The last two of the eight possible kinds of moves, circulation within the core or within the periphery (i.e., moves not transcending the boundaries of core or of periphery), were by far the most common among sample members, accounting for a majority of their moves.

Between 1830 and 1860, the 1540 sample members moved 5742 times. Of this total, 3111 moves, or 54.2 per cent, were circulatory. Most of the moves involved only short distances. In addition to ante-bellum Boston's small size as compared with other large cities—the heart of the city a peninsula about two miles long by one wide—the city was pre-eminently a pedestrian city. Until the latter half of the 1850's, a student of ante-bellum urban transportation concludes, public transportation in Boston was almost exclusively patronized by the middle and upper classes, for omnibus fares were about six cents per trip in an era when laborers earned about a dollar a day.[6] Since laborers did not wish to spend too much time walking to and from work, they tried to live near their work. In 1846, a committee of concerned Bostonians investigated the residential difficulties of the laboring classes, concluding that

> we cannot doubt, that a very large proportion of the day laborers, would pay almost any rents, near their work, rather than move. . . . the *bulk* of the day laborers will, at all events, cluster as near their work as they can get. . . .[7]

These three factors—a small, crowded city, no low-cost public transportation, laborers' desire to rent near their work—combined to create and maintain residential instability among the population, especially among the lower classes. George Adams, who took the state-sponsored census of Boston in May 1850, noted what the expansion of business in Boston's central wards was doing to their residents:

> The returns from the central Wards show the advances made by stores and warehouses upon the former dwellings. This is seen particularly in Wards 2 and 7. Ward 4 has also greatly changed from this cause. . . .
>
> In some portions of the City, . . . the foreign population have of late located themselves, and occupy almost exclusively the dwelling houses. But as those streets are near the business places, it is probable that this population will, before long, be displaced, and stores will take the place of the houses to accommodate the increasing trade of the City.[8]

Expansion of business areas, desire of laborers to live near these areas, increasing rents of buildings near the central business district as it grew, only occasional employment of laborers, their lack of savings—the list could be much extended. Each factor worked against stability of residence among the lower economic orders who were coming, surely, as successive censuses seemed to augur, to dominate the population of Boston. Looking at the question another way, we may compare the loci of circulation with the components which were causing it. Table IV-13 examines the four samples in their most mobile periods, breaking down circulatory moves by native- and foreign-born according to their area of residence. The foreign-born were consistently more active in Boston's core than their proportion there would have warranted, assuming equal city-wide rates. But the converse generally held for the native-born, who circulated more in the periphery than one would anticipate from their proportion living there. The exception was the 1845–49 period, in which Boston experienced the unusually large population movement from the core already mentioned. Since circulatory moves make no impact whatever on census results, circulation acts apart from population influx and efflux. It increases instability, but produces no results that censuses can detect. In ante-bellum Boston it was yet another factor contributing to population instability, particularly among the foreign-born.

Table IV-13. Circulation of Native- and Foreign-Born Sample Members, by Area, Compared with Their Residential Distribution, 1830-1834, 1840-1844, 1845-1849, and 1855-1859.

Sample and Period	*Native-Born*				*Foreign-Born*			
	Per Cent of Circulation in		*Per Cent of Population (Households) in*		*Per Cent of Circulation in*		*Per Cent of Population (Households) in*	
	Core	*Periphery*	*Core*	*Periphery*	*Core*	*Periphery*	*Core*	*Periphery*
1830 during 1830-34	25.2	74.8	33.6	66.4	72.7	27.3	61.9	38.1
1840 during 1840-44	47.1	52.9	53.2	46.8	65.4	34.6	61.8	38.2
1850 during 1845-49	45.1	54.9	43.1	56.9	47.4	52.6	39.8	60.2
1860 during 1855-59	38.4	61.6	43.5	56.5	46.7	53.3	42.3	57.7

Source: Sample data.

Centralization, the movement of persons from periphery to core, and decentralization, the contrary movement, did not account for a large proportion of sample members' moves. Here again is an example of two population movements the full impact of which upon the city's inhabitants went undetected by censuses. Decentralization, or rather *net* decentralization, did come to dominate the over-all picture of population shifts in ante-bellum Boston (*cf.* Table II-8). Nevertheless, this was a census measurement of *net* movement, which did not disclose the amount of centralization occurring simultaneously, except that the latter was less than the total decentralization. It is conceivable that in the antebellum period there occurred very little centralization *per se,* that rather population moved from outside Boston to its core, and thence to the periphery, but the sample results do not confirm this. Instead, they suggest variations in the intensity of both centralization and decentralization over the 30-year period.

Decentralization was at its height in the 1840's, when it accounted for more than 10 per cent of the moves of both the 1840 and 1850 sample members. However, this strong decentralization was to some extent countervailed by a centralizing movement just declining from a maximum in the late 1830's. The sequence, according to the sample data (presented in Table IV-14), was one of increasing decentralization until the later 1840's, then a decline through the 1850's. Centralization peaked earlier, in the late 1830's, then fell off during the 'forties, rose again in the early 'fifties, and fell in the late 'fifties. The resultant of these two opposed population flows was low net decentralization in the 1830's, rising to a maximum in the 'forties, dropping to zero or even becoming negative in the early 1850's, and recovering somewhat in the late 'fifties.

As one might anticipate from a knowledge of foreign-born individuals' high circulation rates, their decentralizing and centralizing rates were usually lower than those of native-born persons; in other words, they were more parochially oriented with respect to residential change. Since native-born persons predominated in the 1830, 1840, and 1850 samples, essentially their

Table IV-14. Decentralizing and Centralizing Moves as Per Cent of All Moves of Total Samples in Various Periods, 1830-1859

Sample and Period	*Total Moves*	*Decentralizing Per Cent*	*Centralizing Per Cent*	*Net Decentralizing Per Cent*
1830 during 1830-34	474	8.9	6.5	2.4
1840 during 1830-34	244	9.8	7.8	2.0
1830 during 1835-39	263	9.1	9.1	–
1840 during 1835-39	484	8.1	7.4	0.7
1840 during 1840-44	466	10.9	6.7	4.2
1850 during 1840-44	202	14.4	6.4	8.0
1840 during 1845-49	303	10.5	4.6	5.9
1850 during 1845-49	506	6.9	3.8	3.1
1850 during 1850-54	446	4.5	5.4	–0.9
1860 during 1850-54	234	6.0	6.0	–
1850 during 1855-59	309	6.5	2.9	3.6
1860 during 1855-59	519	5.2	3.1	2.1

Source: Sample data.

record of centralization and decentralization was the samples' also. But about 1850, a combination of high mobility among foreign-born and their increasing proportion of the city's population meant that their movements came to outnumber those of the native-born (see Table IV-15). The foreign-born led the centralizing movement of the early 'fifties that resulted in net centralization for all sample members during 1850–54. In the next five years, however, the stream reversed and again became a net outward flow.

What, then, does this analysis demonstrate? First it again underlines the importance of distinctions between native- and foreign-born in analyzing population movements. While native-born individuals were consistently (with a possible exception in 1850–54) engaged in a net outward movement during all of the

Table IV-15. Decentralizing and Centralizing Moves as Per Cent of All Moves of Foreign-Born Members of Samples in Various Periods, 1830-1859

Sample and Period	*Total Moves*	*Decentral-izing Per Cent*	*Central-izing Per Cent*	*Net Decentral-izing Per Cent*
1830 during 1830-34	53	11.3	11.3	–
1840 during 1830-34	41	4.9	4.9	–
1830 during 1835-39	28	10.7	7.1	3.6
1840 during 1835-39	92	5.4	4.3	1.1
1840 during 1840-44	82	8.5	7.3	1.2
1850 during 1840-44	48	6.3	–	6.3
1840 during 1845-49	66	15.1	6.1	9.0
1850 during 1845-49	242	5.4	2.5	2.9
1850 during 1850-54	222	3.6	5.4	−1.8
1860 during 1850-54	100	2.0	4.0	−2.0
1850 during 1855-59	152	5.9	2.6	3.3
1860 during 1855-59	318	4.1	1.9	2.2

Source: Sample data.

ante-bellum period, foreign-born sample members again betrayed their attraction toward the core of the city. While it is true that on the whole they too participated in a net outward movement, this trend was arrested during the early 'thirties and reversed in the early 'fifties. Having noted that in 1845–49 there was a strong decentralizing trend on the part of all city residents, one wonders why, given the continued expansion of business in the core of the city, foreigners should relocate there in the early 'fifties after having left in the previous five years. What happened in Boston in 1850–54, in other words, to make it possible for sizable numbers of foreign-born to move back into the central wards of the city? To put the question more broadly, could still other population movements have affected centralization and decentralization?

Unfortunately for those who like simple explanations, the answer appears to be a qualified yes. There are four kinds of population shifts not yet accounted for, in two complementary pairs. They are in-migration and out-migration to and from the core and periphery of the city. Again, assume opposite and equal flows of population between (say) Boston's core and outside the city, or between the periphery and the outside world. Total movement could be considerable, net change inconsiderable. Was that, in fact, the case?

It would seem not. Total movement and net change were both considerable, and they were usually related to centralization and decentralization. For both native- and foreign-born groups, periods of rapid decentralization also witnessed high rates of in-migration to the core. As people moved from the core to the periphery, others, replacing them, shifted from outside Boston to its core. But when centralization was at its height in the early 'thirties, the highest rates of in-migration were to the periphery. The vacancies left at the city's edge were thus filled by newcomers. As for out-migration, it was normally greater from the periphery than from the core. The sole exception occurred during a period of strong centralizing tendencies, when persons quitting the city from the core were replaced by those moving in from the periphery. For each movement, then, there was a complementary or compensating movement taking up the slack of vacated residences.

Along the native-foreign dimension, foreign-born out-migration from the core was, until the late 'fifties, always higher than that from the periphery. But, except for the late 'forties, foreign-born tended to move from outside Boston to its periphery rather than to its core. The "usual" population flow of the foreign-born, then, was from outside Boston to its periphery, a short stay in the periphery, then a shift to the core, circulation within the core, and (after a few years) departure from the core.

The native-born were less consistent in their movements. During the 'thirties, in a period of high centralization, they too tended to move from outside the city into the periphery. But they left the city from core and periphery in about equal numbers.

Table IV-16. In- and Out-Migration, 1830-1859, of Total Samples, of Native-Born, and of Foreign-Born, as Per Cent of All Their Moves

Sample and Period	Total Moves	In-Migration to (Per Cent)		Out-Migration from (Per Cent)	
		Core	Periphery	Core	Periphery
TOTAL SAMPLES					
1830 during 1830-34	474	–	–	11.4	18.6
1840 during 1830-34	244	10.7	13.9	–	–
1830 during 1835-39	263	–	–	12.6	15.6
1840 during 1835-39	484	17.2	17.5	–	–
1840 during 1840-44	466	–	–	14.8	11.4
1850 during 1840-44	202	14.9	10.4	–	–
1840 during 1845-49	303	–	–	14.5	12.2
1850 during 1845-49	506	17.0	24.1	–	0.4[a]
1850 during 1850-54	446	–	0.2[b]	18.9	14.9
1860 during 1850-54	234	10.3	15.8	1.4[a]	1.6[a]
1850 during 1855-59	309	0.9[b]	1.0[b]	13.6	15.8
1860 during 1855-59	519	17.0	18.7	0.4[a]	0.2[a]
NATIVE-BORN					
1830 during 1830-34	161	–	–	5.0	5.6
1840 during 1830-34	126	11.9	15.1	–	–
1830 during 1835-39	110	–	–	4.5	4.5
1840 during 1835-39	230	10.4	11.3	–	–
1840 during 1840-44	207	–	–	6.3	4.3
1850 during 1840-44	154	11.0	11.7	–	–
1840 during 1845-49	174	1.2[b]	0.6[b]	7.5	7.5
1850 during 1845-49	264	10.5	13.7	–	–
1850 during 1850-54	224	–	0.4[b]	18.2	14.7
1860 during 1850-54	134	6.0	13.4	2.2[a]	2.2[a]
1850 during 1855-59	157	2.0[b]	0.6[b]	13.4	15.9
1860 during 1855-59	201	13.5	11.5	1.0[a]	–

			FOREIGN-BORN		
1830 during 1830-34	53	–	–	24.5	11.3
1840 during 1830-34	41	14.6	14.6	–	–
1830 during 1835-39	28	–	–	17.8	3.6
1840 during 1835-39	92	23.9	25.0	–	–
1840 during 1840-44	82	–	–	13.4	7.3
1850 during 1840-44	48	29.1	6.3	–	–
1840 during 1845-49	66	–	–	12.1	4.6
1850 during 1845-49	242	24.4	35.5	–	–
1850 during 1850-54	222	–	–	19.8	14.9
1860 during 1850-54	100	16.0	19.0	–	1.0[a]
1850 during 1855-59	152	–	1.3[b]	13.8	15.8
1860 during 1855-59	318	19.2	23.3	–	0.3[a]

For the 1830 and 1840 samples, the total of native-born and foreign-born moves does not equal that of the total sample because of the presence in those samples of persons of unknown ethnic background.

[a]These figures represent persons who out-migrated, but later returned and were included in the sample at its census year.

[b]These figures represent persons who left Boston after their sample's census year, but later returned.

Source: Sample data.

From the 'forties to the mid-'fifties, native Americans continued to prefer entering the city at the periphery. However, their core out-migration rates rose above the peripheral out-migration rates. They were tending to leave Boston from its core rather than from its periphery. In the late 'fifties, both trends reversed: the native-born tended to move from outside Boston to its core, and to depart from the city's outskirts. For the 'thirties then, native-born persons tended to arrive in Boston's periphery. Not many of them moved inward; most circulated instead in the periphery. They left the city about equally from the core and from the periphery. By the 'forties and early 'fifties, native-born continued to prefer moving from outside Boston to its fringes, where they tended to circulate. Those native-born who did centralize, and others who already lived in central areas, started leaving Boston from the core in greater numbers. Foreigners were centralizing and moving from outside Boston to the core to replace them. By the late 'fifties, with foreign-born continuing to enter the city, particularly at the edges, natives began preferring to move from outside Boston to the core. Their net decentralization rates fell off, and by the late 'fifties the number of adult native-born in the core area may have been increasing again (see Table IV-16).

Unfortunately for those who wish a sure grasp of all population changes in ante-bellum Boston, all of the population movements producing net change (decentralization, centralization, core and peripheral in- and out-migration) are overlain by yet other vital mechanisms, those of birth and death. Since Boston's birth records are fragmentary until 1849, and since its death records are little, if any, better, it would be extremely difficult to gauge the areal population changes these forces brought about. For the present we must remain content with what we have learned about the movements of household heads.

The eight kinds of population movements reviewed included two (circulation in core and periphery) that did not contribute to net population changes. The other six operated to increase Boston's population differentially, as revealed by the city's censuses. Rather than an overwhelming population shift, or lemming-like scurry, as the censuses suggest, Boston's considerable peripheral growth in the ante-bellum era was the resultant of three opposed pairs or streams of population flow. In-migration to the periphery (except in the early '40's) always slightly exceeded in-migration to the core. Decentralization (except in the early '50's) always slightly exceeded centralization. Less consistently, out-migration from the core usually outweighed that from the periphery. Here the excepted periods were the 'thirties and the late 'fifties. In both these latter periods net decentralization and excess of peripheral over core in-migration assured the continued faster growth of the periphery.

Taken together, the eight population movements make up general population mobility. It may be worthwhile to see whether there seem to exist any as yet unnoted reciprocal relationships among the population shifts. We have already seen that when centralization was high, in-migration to the periphery rose. Similarly, in times of high decentralization, out-migration from the core increased. These findings are consistent if one postulates that in ante-bellum Boston there were only so many dwellings for people to occupy, i.e., the population could change much more quickly than accommodations for it could be built. For practical purposes the supply of housing at any moment was static. Thus, as persons centralized, they left vacancies in the periphery, while filling them in the core. Newcomers accordingly found accommodation more easily at the periphery, where presumably rents were also lower, an additional attraction. When decentralization was high, however, so were core out-migration of all sample members and core circulation of foreign-born. This development is consistent with a decrease or slow relative increase of housing in Boston's core area. Contemporary accounts, one of which was quoted earlier, agree with this analysis that as businesses expanded into what had been residential areas, native-born persons, presumably generally of higher socioeconomic status than most of the foreign-born, decentralized or left the city (this trend will be considered in Chapter VI). Foreigners thus displaced by expanding business and commercial needs presumably still wished to live near their work; they shifted residence within the core, increasing their circulatory rate. This situation did not last long, for by the late 'forties foreigners were tending to decentralize. With continuing business construction in the core, one may theorize that by the early 'fifties, real estate owners there saw increased profits to be gained from subdividing larger residences once occupied by the well-to-do native-born; these residences could then be let to foreign-born workers seeking to live near their work, as had been done in the area just south of the central business district in the late 'forties. The native-born, who in the early 'fifties had lived in the core, were shifting out of Boston. This development also was short-lived, for the trend reversed again by the late 'fifties, and native-born began displacing the foreign-born in the core again. Interestingly, several of the study's sample members who participated in this operation had moved to the suburbs about 1850, only to return to Boston after a few years. It may be that commutation by railroad was too arduous for them.

Since circulatory moves (those within the core or periphery) accounted for more than half of the sample members' moves, times of high circulation were also times of high mobility. Table IV-17 shows that circulation was most intense during the 'fifties. Simultaneously, though, centralization and decentralization were both low, while quite a few persons were entering and leaving Boston from the core and periphery. Movement was not so much

Table IV-17. Circulation Moves, 1830-1859, as Per Cent of All Moves of Total Sample, of Native-Born, and of Foreign-Born

	Total Sample		*Native-Born*		*Foreign-Born*	
Sample and Period	*Total Moves*	*Circ. (%)*	*Total Moves*	*Circ. (%)*	*Total Moves*	*Circ. (%)*
1830 during 1830-34	474	54.6	161	68.9	53	41.5
1840 during 1830-34	244	58.2	126	60.3	41	61.0
1830 during 1835-39	263	53.6	110	70.0	28	60.7
1840 during 1835-39	484	49.8	230	59.6	92	41.3
1840 during 1840-44	466	56.2	207	66.7	82	63.4
1850 during 1840-44	202	53.5	154	52.0	48	56.3
1840 during 1845-49	303	56.4	174	66.1	66	62.1
1850 during 1845-49	506	47.8	264	61.8	242	32.2
1850 during 1850-54	446	56.2	224	56.0	222	56.3
1860 during 1850-54	234	59.0	134	59.7	100	58.0
1850 during 1855-59	309	59.2	157	58.0	152	60.5
1860 during 1855-59	519	55.5	201	62.5	318	51.2

For the 1830 and 1840 samples, the total of native-born and foreign-born moves does not equal that of the total sample because of the presence in those samples of persons of unknown ethnic background.

Source: Sample data.

across boundaries within Boston, as within those boundaries and to and from the city. In other words, the parochial nature of core and periphery had intensified by the 'fifties. A "hardening" of residential areas had occurred, despite an apparent resurgence of native-born toward the core after 1855. Changing residential patterns were tending to divide Boston into sub-communities.

Without much more extensive research into the economic and spatial structure of ante-bellum Boston, it would be foolhardy to speculate beyond what has already been said about the *causes* of the various kinds of population movements just discussed. The movements may have been due largely to rent differentials or transportation cost differentials; if so, the necessary corroborative data appear, for the moment, to be beyond recovery. There is some indication of self-segregation of foreign-born in the core and native-born at the periphery, and of displacement of the native-born by foreign-born (in the core until about 1854) and *vice versa* (in the core after about 1854).

It is worth keeping in mind, then, that almost all of the population movements we have been considering are "phantom" movements in that censuses detect them imperfectly if at all; that the movements fluctuated over time but gradually increased in scope because of the growing dominance in the population of the more mobile and less persistent foreign-born; and that Boston's population growth, as analyzed here, was the resultant of six different population flows and of two natural processes (births and deaths), while it was affected by two other kinds of population redistribution (circulation in core and periphery).

The sample members possessed characteristics other than those of "country of birth," of course, and it may well have been that (say) their economic success, or lack of it, affected their residential choice. If this is so, we would anticipate finding that more successful persons possessed certain residential characteristics distinguishing them from the less successful.

V

Wealth Trends in Ante-Bellum Boston

Another cause [besides intemperance] of the pauperism existing here is Immigration, aggravated greatly by the unwillingness of certain portions of the immigrants to leave the city, thereby causing a large surplus of laborers, or of persons without permanent employment; and also by the fact, that, generally speaking, the most enterprising and thrifty seek the country, or the far West, immediately on their arrival here, and leave the shiftless behind.

BOSTON SOCIETY FOR THE PREVENTION OF PAUPERISM[1]

The frugality which characterizes the old Bay State is the great secret of accumulation. Here every artisan aspires to own his house, and to leave a patrimony to his children. Having secured his dwelling, he buys a single share in a bank, railway, or factory, and gradually becomes a capitalist.

ELIAS H. DERBY[2]

The increased competition for employment has diminished the facility of obtaining it, and reduced the compensation for labor. In many employments the foreigners, at first compelled by necessity to labor for small wages, have at length almost excluded the natives. . . . it may be questioned how far the *average* comfort has been increased, and whether . . . the *average* value of real wealth and means . . . is as great as it would have been without this addition [to Massachusetts] of nearly 200,000 of foreign population during the last twenty years.

JESSE CHICKERING[3]

Elias Hasket Derby, quoted above, was in no position to serve as an inspiration to struggling artisans. A good part of his wealth was inherited, and he multiplied it well. His 1830 Boston city tax assessment of $3000 rose to $70,400 ten years later. When he wrote about aspiring artisans in mid-1850, he had just paid the tax on a city assessment of $43,000.[4] (Presumably the decline was a result of Derby's extensive—and non-taxed—railroad investments after the mid-'forties.[5]) But his statement should be taken as expressing an opinion supposedly widespread at the time: a man could start low and end high.[6] The careers of some of Boston's eminent men seemed to hold out this promise. In the generally prosperous latter half of the 1840's, a new genre of books appeared, describing men of wealth. Works such as *"Our First Men:" A Calendar of Wealth, Fashion and Gentility . . .*,[7] *The Aristocracy of Boston; Who They Are, and What They Were . . .*,[8] and *The Rich Men of Massachusetts . . .*[9] suggested that perhaps the reader too, with good fortune, might rise to the top of the heap. Could anyone perusing, say, *The Rich Men of Massachusetts,* have missed the display on page 14, where thirteen prominent businessmen, from Bancroft, Jacob, to Bates, Martin, were assigned total assets of $2.3 million? And of the thirteen, ten "started poor" or "commenced poor." Of course, two of the ten married rich, but that still left eight of the thirteen who had begun with modest means.

Those who write of "success" in other than a qualitative way are condemned to define the term. This presents a thoroughly uncongenial task for one who, though aware of the pervasiveness of the "success" ethos in historical sources, yet harbors doubts as to the penetration of that ethos to the layers of Boston's society here uncovered. Since ante-bellum Bostonians are not available for interviews designed to elicit their concepts of "success," this study uses an economic measure of advancement based on changes in individuals' real and personal property assessments (in current dollars) over ten-year periods. At least four difficulties inherent in this method immediately spring to mind. First, the method ignores the matter of prestige as a very real contributing factor in "success." Then, what of the extensive mobility of Boston's population? Too, the dollar's buying power fluctuated during 1830–

60. Last, if Boston's property was assessed by different men in different parts of town at yearly intervals, and if those assessments are compiled and compared for this study only at ten-year intervals, does there not arise a serious question as to the comparability of individuals' assessments over time?

At this distance in time, the question of prestige appears to be insoluble. It seems safe to conclude that Bostonians ascribed greater prestige to professional persons than to unskilled laborers, but what of, say, a butcher as against a messenger, or a sailor as against a sawyer? Nevertheless, this study does employ a socioeconomic ranking scheme (elucidated later in this chapter) to measure occupational mobility. The principal virtue of the ranking scheme is its use in another study of Boston, 1880–1968, now nearing completion; this will permit (admittedly imperfect) mobility comparisons with early nineteenth-century Boston.

Quantitative changes in property assessments were measured at decadal intervals. The study design had been established and all data collected before evaluation of the residential information revealed general annual residential mobility rates of about 40 per cent and interdecadal persistence rates approximating 40 per cent. Only "persisters'" property assessments could be measured at start and finish of a decade,[10] so "success" was biased toward the persistent. Ideally, property measurements should have been gathered for the study at five-year intervals, thus including many more of the less persistent Bostonians.

Modern studies of nineteenth-century economic data permit calculation of the dollar's purchasing power at various times. Converting one such purchasing power index to 1860 dollars shows that during 1830–60 the dollar bought from 85 cents' (1837) to $1.20 (1834, 1843, 1849) worth of goods in terms of the 1860 dollar. The 1830 and 1850 dollar were worth $1.13 in 1860 dollars, while the 1840 dollar was estimated at $1.02 in 1860 terms.[11] Despite these changes, all dollar values in this study, unless otherwise stated, are given in current, unadjusted dollars. There are two reasons for this. First, even in hard times, Boston's assessors tended to keep individuals' assessments at the same level regardless of the dollar's changed buying power, while the city-wide total advanced from year to year. Since the assessment totals of American cities achieved wide circulation and were used as indicators of city growth, the assessors may have wished to demonstrate to residents of other cities that Boston was doing well even in the face of adversity. The city's property assessment total declined only twice during 1830–60: in 1851–52 and in 1857–58.[12] The per capita assessment rose from $971 in 1830 to $1560 in 1860, or from $1098 to $1560 in 1860 dollars, an advance of 42.1 per cent in "real" terms. This study follows the assessors' practice of not adjusting for changing dollar purchasing power.

A second, and probably stronger, rationale for leaving dollars in current or unadjusted amounts dovetails with the last of the problems that sprang to mind in determining "success": the question of non-uniform city-wide assessment. Each ward's assessment practices varied from those of the other wards. In fact, concluded a City Council committee in 1842,

> By the present system, the Assessors of a ward, come to be considered and to consider themselves, as officers of the ward,—appointed to look after the interest of their ward, which interest is to keep down the valuation in the ward. It accordingly may happen that in a street which constitutes the boundary between two wards, estates upon one side are valued one third more or less than those of really the same value upon the other side, because the valuations are fixed by different men in the two cases.[13]

In addition, valuations of individuals' personal (as distinct from real) property were made, under oath if necessary, by the individuals themselves, opening yet another door to error.

Accordingly, this study adopted a very modest definition of "success." If, over a ten-year period following the census year in which he was chosen as a sample member, an individual increased his total assessment (in current dollars), he was deemed "successful." If his assessment remained constant or decreased (again, in current dollars), he was classified as "unsuccessful." This definition, be it remembered, is thus biased toward persistence of residence in Boston. If only 40 per cent of a population remains in a city ten years after a census, obviously one will not be able to conclude that more than 40 per cent of the original group was "successful" or "unsuccessful."

This chapter considers the question of "success" from three viewpoints: first, occupational or socioeconomic groups in general; second, individual wealth at the start of each of the three ante-bellum decades; and last, persons who happen to fall into the various occupational groupings. This threefold approach permits a reasonably thorough consideration of an individual's chances of becoming better off in ante-bellum Boston. Since "success" was partially related to the socioeconomic status of individuals, it is helpful to delineate some of the changes which occurred in the various socioeconomic groups during the ante-bellum years. As one might anticipate, the structure of Boston's activities was changing then; thus an individual, member of an economically declining occupational group, might well have been disadvantaged in his climb to riches as compared with one fortunate enough to have joined a rising group.

What is meant by "group" in this context? In the evaluation of data collected for this study, individuals have been grouped, primarily upon an occupational basis, in an effort to classify, quantify, and interpret some of the flux that was ante-bellum Boston. The scheme of classification was developed by a scholar currently investigating Boston in the period 1880–1968, and was adopted here to make the two studies comparable as far as socioeconomic categories were concerned.[14] The system divides most of society into eight principal groups: Unskilled & Menial Service; Semi-Skilled & Service; Petty Proprietors, Managers, & Officials (with less than $1000 in personal property, less than $5000 total property*); Skilled; Clerical & Sales; Semi-Professional; Proprietors, Managers, & Officials (with over $1000 in personal property and over $5000 total property*); and Professional.**

* In the present study, the property cut-off has been lowered to $1000 for *total* property, regardless of whether real or personal.

** A complete listing of all occupations in each category is in Appendix E.

Since the classification deals only with employed members of society, a ninth division, Miscellaneous & Unknown, was added for the purposes of the present study, which comprehends a sample of all of Boston's heads of household, regardless of employment status. (Some 231 of the 1540 sample members were females; most of them were not employed, in any formal sense. They, together with retired men and persons of unknown occupation, made up the Miscellaneous & Unknown category.)

In the ante-bellum period, the most prominent alteration in the socioeconomic distribution of Boston's population was the marked increase of persons in the Unskilled & Menial Service category. The proportion of household heads in this group had risen slightly in the 1830's, from 11.4 per cent to 14.3 per cent, but this was completely overshadowed by the growth of the 1840's—to 27.0 per cent. By 1860 the figure had slipped to 22.1 per cent. Translating these proportions into estimated absolute numbers gives a better idea of the classification's growth. From an estimated 1085 heads of household included in the Unskilled & Menial Service group as of 1830, the totals rose to 2010 in 1840, to 6660 in 1850, and to 7430 by 1860. This represented about a 230 per cent increase for the 'forties, compared with only 85 per cent in the 'thirties and 10 per cent for the 'fifties.

Those heads of household who were Skilled added nearly 4000 to their ranks during the 'forties, rising from about 2560 in 1840 to around 6260 by 1850. They had numbered about 1875 in 1830, and grew to 6820 in 1860. Thus, by 1850 the skilled and unskilled workers together made up 52.4 per cent of the city's heads of household. They gained relatively at the expense of the administrative groups—the Petty and larger-scale Proprietors, Managers, & Officials, whose numbers are estimated to have declined somewhat in the 1840's, from roughly 5575 to 5270.

In view of Boston's rapid population growth during the 'forties, one would rightly anticipate that various occupational groups made their greatest numerical gains in that decade. Clerical & Sales workers who headed households more than tripled in number from 1840 to 1850 and almost tripled again in the 'fifties.

Table V-1. Estimated Numbers of Household Heads in Various Socioeconomic Groups, and Per Cent Decadal Change in Size of Those Groups, Boston, 1830-1860

Socio-economic Group[a]	*1830* *Estimated Household Heads in Category*	*Per Cent Change, 1830-1840*	*1840* *Estimated Household Heads in Category*	*Per Cent Change, 1840-1850*	*1850* *Estimated Household Heads in Category*	*Per Cent Change, 1850-1860*	*1860* *Estimated Household Heads in Category*
1	1085	85	2010	230	6660	10	7430
2	790	10	875	55	1350	140	3230
3	1580	45	2330	5	2450	20	2880
4	1875	35	2560	145	6260	10	6820
5	220	35	290	225	960	170	2620
6	170	30	225	– 15	190	– 5	175
7	1385	125	3245	– 15	2820	90	5420
8	340	– 15	290	185	830	– 15	700
9 SW	1285	15	1495	80	2690	40	3845
9 RM	340	– 25	255	75	450	15	525
9 UO	450	5	475	–100[b]	–	–	–
Total estimate	9520	48	14,050	76	24,660	36	33,645
Actual Total	9518		14,047		24,667		33,633
City Population	61,392	39	85,000	61	136,884	30	177,840

[a]1=Unskilled & Menial; 2=Semi-Skilled & Service; 3=Petty Proprietors, Managers, & Officials; 4=Skilled; 5=Clerical & Sales; 6=Semi-Professional; 7=Proprietors, Managers, & Officials; 8=Professional; 9 SW=Single Women; 9 RM=Retired Men; 9 UO=Unknown Occupation.

[b]In and after 1850, all household heads' occupations were listed in the manuscript federal census.

Source: Sample data. Estimates were rounded off to the nearest five.

Where perhaps 220 had been so classified in 1830, about 2620 qualified in 1860. Unskilled & Menial workers, and those in the Skilled, Clerical & Sales, and Professional categories all outpaced the growth of the total workforce in the 1840's. For the Skilled and Professional groups this was the only decade in which their growth rate ran ahead of that of the total population. In the case of Professionals, the change meant that Boston's people were, in per capita terms, less and less well served by them except during the 'forties. During the 'fifties the number of Professionals appears to have declined absolutely as well as relatively (see Table V-1).

Members of the occupational classifications were variously distributed during the ante-bellum era. Owing to the considerable population shifts going on, few groups remained consistently concentrated at either core or periphery throughout the whole period. Professionals were concentrated disproportionately in the city's core during all three decades. Other locational trends of occupational groups were less clear. Unskilled & Menial Service workers were centrally concentrated in 1830 and 1840, but by 1850 were rather uniformly distributed; in 1860 they tended to concentrate in the periphery. This is consistent with the marked Irish preponderance within the group (*cf.* Chapter IV). Semi-Skilled & Service workers, on the other hand, tended to centralize after having been uniformly distributed throughout the city in 1830 and 1840. Skilled Bostonians preferred peripheral areas except in 1840, when they were spread more evenly throughout.

Persons in the Clerical & Sales group tended to live in outlying areas until after 1840, when they centralized. Large-scale Proprietors, Managers, & Officials manifested no particular concentration until after 1850, when they decentralized. Their Petty brethren dispersed earlier: from a central concentration as of 1830, they spread outward, achieving a peripheral concentration by 1840 and maintaining it (see Table V-2).

Which occupational and socioeconomic groups fared better or worse in pre-Civil War Boston? During the 'thirties, members of the Professional group were about two and one-half times as

Table V-2. Central and Peripheral Residence of Various Socioeconomic Groups, Boston, 1830-1860 (Sample Data)

Socio-economic Group[a]	1830			1840		
	Core	*Periphery*	*Per Cent of Total*	*Core*	*Periphery*	*Per Cent of Total*
1	45.5	54.5	11.4	67.2	32.8	14.3
(N)	(20)	(24)	(44)	(37)	(18)	(55)
2	34.4	65.6	8.3	62.5	37.5	6.2
(N)	(11)	(21)	(32)	(15)	(9)	(24)
3	48.4	51.6	16.6	53.1	46.9	16.6
(N)	(31)	(33)	(64)	(34)	(30)	(64)
4	26.3	73.7	19.7	57.1	42.9	18.2
(N)	(20)	(56)	(76)	(40)	(30)	(70)
5	22.2	77.8	2.3	25.0	75.0	2.1
(N)	(2)	(7)	(9)	(2)	(6)	(8)
6	42.9	57.1	1.8	83.3	16.7	1.6
(N)	(3)	(4)	(7)	(5)	(1)	(6)
7	34.0	66.0	14.5	53.9	46.1	23.1
(N)	(19)	(37)	(56)	(48)	(41)	(89)
8	50.0	50.0	3.6	75.0	25.0	2.1
(N)	(7)	(7)	(14)	(6)	(2)	(8)
9 SW	(33.3)	66.7	13.2	61.0	39.0	10.6
(N)	(17)	(34)	(51)	(25)	(16)	(41)
9 RM	(42.9)	57.1	3.6	42.9	57.1	1.8
(N)	(6)	(8)	(14)	(3)	(4)	(7)
9 UO	50.0	50.0	4.7	54.8	45.2	3.4
(N)	(9)	(9)	(18)	(7)	(6)	(13)
Sample Total	37.7	62.3	99.7	57.7	42.3	100.0
(N)	(145)	(240)	(385)	(222)	(163)	(385)
House-holds	37.3	62.7	100.0	58.4	41.6	100.0
(N)	(3552)	(5966)	(9518)	(8198)	(5849)	(14,047)
Census	41.4	58.6	100.0	57.4	42.6	100.0
(N)	(25,416)	(35,976)	(61,392)	(48,776)	(36,224)	(85,000)

Socio-economic Group[a]	1850			1860		
	Core	Periphery	Per Cent of Total	Core	Periphery	Per Cent of Total
1	41.3	58.7	27.0	36.4	63.6	22.1
(N)	(43)	(61)	(104)	(31)	(54)	(85)
2	47.7	52.3	5.5	64.9	35.1	9.6
(N)	(10)	(11)	(21)	(24)	(13)	(37)
3	29.0	71.0	9.9	33.3	66.7	8.6
(N)	(11)	(27)	(38)	(11)	(22)	(33)
4	35.7	64.3	25.5	32.0	68.0	20.3
(N)	(35)	(63)	(98)	(25)	(53)	(78)
5	73.3	26.7	3.9	56.7	43.3	7.8
(N)	(11)	(4)	(15)	(17)	(13)	(30)
6	66.7	33.3	0.8	100.0	–	0.5
(N)	(2)	(1)	(3)	(2)	(–)	(2)
7	40.9	59.1	11.4	33.9	66.1	16.1
(N)	(18)	(26)	(44)	(21)	(41)	(62)
8	54.8	45.2	3.4	62.5	37.5	2.1
(N)	(7)	(6)	(13)	(5)	(3)	(8)
9 SW	52.3	47.7	10.9	52.2	47.8	11.4
(N)	(22)	(20)	(42)	(23)	(21)	(44)
9 RM	14.3	85.7	1.8	83.3	16.7	1.6
(N)	(1)	(6)	(7)	(5)	(1)	(6)
9 OU	–[b]	–[b]	–[b]	–[b]	–[b]	–[b]
(N)	–[b]	–[b]	–[b]	–[b]	–[b]	–[b]
Sample Total	41.6	58.4	100.0	42.6	57.4	100.0
(N)	(160)	(225)	(385)	(164)	(221)	(385)
House-holds	41.2	58.8	100.0	42.6	57.4	100.0
(N)	(10,172)	(14,495)	(24,667)	(14,330)	(19,303)	(33,633)
Census	41.9	58.1	100.0	43.0	57.0	100.0
(N)	(57,284)	(79,600)	(136,884)	(76,455)	(101,385)	(177,840)

[a] 1=Unskilled & Menial; 2=Semi-Skilled & Service; 3=Petty Proprietors, Managers, & Officials; 4=Skilled; 5=Clerical & Sales; 6=Semi-Professional; 7=Proprietors, Managers, & Officials; 8=Professional; 9 SW=Single Women; 9 RM=Retired Men; 9 UO=Unknown Occupation.

[b] In and after 1850, all household heads' occupations were listed in the manuscript federal census.

Source: Sample data.

likely to advance their wealth holdings as they were to remain at the same level or to fall behind. Clerical & Sales personnel enjoyed a two-to-one advantage, and Petty Proprietors, Managers, & Officials almost as much. On the other side of the coin, persons in the Semi-Skilled & Service group were about eight times as likely to have kept the same assessment or to have fallen behind as they were to have advanced. Skilled workers were on the unfavorable side of a two-to-one ratio.

By the 'forties, the divergence between advancing and stationary or declining groups was much more pronounced than before. The advance:decline or "no change" ratio among Professionals had risen to about three and one-half to one, while that of Proprietors, Managers, & Officials was up to about two to one (from 1.2 to one). Clerical & Sales' and Petty Proprietors, Managers, & Officials' ratios remained about the same. Changes on the unfavorable side were striking. There the ratios of "non-success" ran from six to one for Unskilled & Menial Service workers (who had been about 1.25 to one), through four to one for Semi-Professionals (formerly about 1.2 to one), to two and one-half to one for Semi-Skilled & Service and Skilled.

During the 1850's the gap between "successful" and "unsuccessful" (including stationary) groups narrowed slightly. Professionals, for instance, actually showed an unfavorable ratio of about 1.1 to one, as did Petty Proprietors, Managers, & Officials. The chances were slightly against their advancing during the decade. But major Proprietors, Managers, & Officials improved their standing, to about a two-and-one-half-to-one ratio of "successes" to "non-successes." The gain among Clerical & Sales workers was noteworthy: from two to one in the 'forties to six to one in the 'fifties. On the debit side, most ratios hovered at about two to one; this held for the Unskilled & Menial, Semi-Skilled & Service, and Skilled groups. No "unfavorable" values were much above two to one.

As far as "success" can be said to apply to occupational or socioeconomic groups, then, disparities between the groups higher and lower on the classification scheme were widening from 1830 till about 1850, after which they tended to diminish. Without entirely disclosing the linkages between "non-success" and out-migration from Boston, to be discussed in the next chapter, we may note generally that the only group which was "successful" and which also showed above-average residential persistence was that of Proprietors, Managers, & Officials (till about 1850). The only markedly "unsuccessful" group with lower than average persistence, as one might guess, was that of Unskilled & Menial workers (after about 1840). Otherwise, it was difficult to differentiate among the "successful," the static, and the "unsuccessful," as to relative propensity to quit Boston.

If there seems to be little apparent pattern in the gains and losses of these occupational groups, it is because the magnification of our retrospective examination is too high: we see trees but not groves. The distribution of property assessments, for example, despite the extensive occupational and residential changes of the ante-bellum period, remained quite stable from 1840 to 1860. Arbitrarily dividing property assessments into four groups according to size of assessment, we have a group of persons who paid only a poll tax, hence owned less than $200 in property (called Group I). Persons who possessed property valued at from $200 to $1000 will be referred to as Group II. Those with property worth from $1001 to $10,000 fall into our Group III, while Group IV will include persons assessed for a total of over $10,000. This approximate division into lower, lower middle, upper middle, and upper classes will roughly represent general "class" distribution within ante-bellum Boston.

In terms of their proportion of all persons assessed, the members of Group I (poll tax only) were concentrated in the periphery in 1830; thereafter, in the core. Persons in Group II ($200–$1000 in property) tended to cluster at the core in 1830 and at the periphery later on. Group III ($1001–$10,000 property valuation) remained peripherally concentrated throughout 1830–60. The wealthiest persons, with assessments of over $10,000 (Group IV), concentrated at the city's core, except that in 1840 they were more or less uniformly distributed. Thus, Boston presented its strongest contrasts in its central areas, where its poorest and its very richest citizens congregated. The poor, as the Committee on the Expediency of Providing Better Tenements for the Poor learned in 1846, had little choice; they had to live near their work (*cf.* Chapter IV). The very rich could escape the central city in the summer, enjoying the residential amenities of the suburbs. In comparison, the city's outlying areas were dominated by the "middle classes," who possessed property valued at from $200 to $10,000.

Most of those in Group I were members of the Skilled and Unskilled & Menial Service categories, while Group II was made up largely of Petty Proprietors, Managers, & Officials. Group III included almost entirely major Proprietors, Managers, & Officials. These usually were in the ascendant in Group IV, but with a strong admixture of Professionals (see Table V-3).

Looking at the four assessment groups as groups, it appears that while the median age of persons in Group II rose slightly in the 30-year period, the corresponding ages for Groups I, III, and IV showed no consistent trend. The median age of non-assessed persons, though, declined sharply, from 44.7 years in 1830, through 40.0 in 1840 and 36.5 in 1850, to 34.7 in 1860. This suggests a marked improvement in assessing procedures in that more and more of the older population were being assessed for some amount, however small.

The median ages for all sample members were 39.9 years in 1830; 38.6 in 1840; 37.2 in 1850; and 38.6 in 1860. When one divides these ages into those for the respective assessment groups, he sees that members of assessment Groups II and IV consistently increased in age faster than did all sample members, indicating increased difficulty of access to Groups II and IV over the antebellum period. The results for Groups I and III were mixed, while the ratios of median ages for non-assessed sample members declined consistently; as assessment improved, it became more usual to rank among the non-assessed.

Over the thirty years, members of the assessment groups tended ever less to move upward from one group to another, varied little in the "no change" classification, and, of course, were more and more likely to drop from higher to lower assessment groups. Less and less often did one see members of Groups I and II vaulting into Group IV during a decade, while by the 1850's fully one-fifth of the Group IV members of 1850 who remained to 1860 had slipped to Group III. The upward and downward paths both became slicker with the years, while the middle way stayed virtually unchanged. Table V-4 summarizes the mobility experiences of the four assessment groups.

Thus, amid the remarkable population turnover and redistribution analyzed in the preceding chapter, some stability of residential and assessment group characteristics did persist. This would suggest that many areas of Boston must have maintained their basic character over the entire ante-bellum period. In other words, while the actors were replaced many times, while the stage was rebuilt, the basic socioeconomic structure of the city remained relatively unaltered, as far as the relationship of core and periphery was concerned. This does not preclude changes' having occurred in individual sub-areas or neighborhoods (as in fact we know they did), but indicates that such changes were usually counterbalanced elsewhere in the core or periphery.

Individuals toiled and moved, but a vague over-all structure persisted. Movement within this structure was not only spatial, but socioeconomic as well. Some people moved up the ladder, others down. In determining who "succeeded" in ante-bellum Boston, the observer must keep in mind several qualifications. First, the only measurement of "success" available to this study was a purely financial one—an individual's property, real and personal, as gauged by the city assessors. The assessors, as far as can be learned,[15] did not take into account property owned outside Boston (suburban real estate, ships, cargoes) or intangible property such as shares in manufacturing corporations. It likewise seems doubtful that they taxed savings accounts (such records have been destroyed or are currently closed). As far as the well-to-do are concerned, then, their wealth is probably understated. Second, since the assessors' records were combed before any mo-

Table V-3. Socioeconomic Composition of the Four Property Assessment Groups, by Per Cent, 1830-1860

—	Socioeconomic Group (by Number)[a]											
	1	*2*	*3*	*4*	*5*	*6*	*7*	*8*	*9 SW*	*9RM*	*Total No.*	*Median Ages*
1830												
Group I (Under $200)	23.4	21.1	6.3	44.5	2.3	—	—	—	—	2.3	(128)	36.9
Group II ($200-$1000)	1.7	1.7	66.7	1.7	10.0	8.3	1.7	3.3	1.7	3.3	(60)	36.3
Group III ($1001-$10,000)	—	—	—	—	—	—	84.0	14.0	2.0	—	(50)	41.3
Group IV (Over $10,000)	—	—	—	—	—	—	63.2	15.8	10.5	10.5	(19)	50.0
1840												
Group I (Under $200)	30.0	15.0	2.5	48.4	0.8	0.8	0.8	0.8	—	0.8	(120)	36.9
Group II ($200-$1000)	2.7	2.7	69.8	—	8.2	5.5	5.5	4.1	—	1.4	(73)	37.1
Group III ($1001-$10,000)	—	—	1.4	—	1.4	—	89.2	4.1	1.4	2.7	(74)	39.8
Group IV (Over $10,000)	—	—	—	—	—	—	85.7	4.8	4.8	4.8	(21)	50.0

1850												
Group I												
(Under $200)	26.6	11.2	3.5	46.9	8.4	1.4	0.7	0.7	—	0.7	(143)	35.2
Group II												
($200-$1000)	13.9	—	72.2	2.8	2.8	—	—	—	5.6	—	(36)	37.3
Group III												
($1001-$10,000)	2.6	—	2.6	5.1	—	—	74.3	5.1	10.3	—	(39)	42.5
Group IV												
(Over $10,000)	—	—	—	—	3.2	—	38.7	25.8	12.9	19.4	(31)	48.4
1860												
Group I												
(Under $200)	23.2	15.5	4.2	40.1	12.7	0.7	0.7	1.4	1.4	—	(142)	37.7
Group II												
($200-$1000)	19.2	—	65.4	—	3.8	—	—	7.7	—	—	(26)	39.3
Group III												
($1001-$10,000)	2.0	—	2.0	2.0	10.0	—	78.0	2.0	4.0	—	(50)	43.6
Group IV												
(Over $10,000)	—	—	—	—	2.9	—	55.9	8.8	17.6	15.2	(34)	55.0

[a] 1=Unskilled & Menial Service; 2=Semi-Skilled & Service; 3=Petty Proprietors, Managers, & Officials; 4=Skilled; 5=Clerical & Sales; 6=Semi-Professional; 7=Proprietors, Managers, & Officials; 8=Professional; 9 SW=Single Women; 9 RM=Retired Men.

Source: Sample data.

Table V-4. Movement and Persistence of Assessment Group Members, 1830-1840, 1840-1850, and 1850-1860

Assessment Group[a], 1830, and Number in Group	*Assessment Group in 1840 of Those Persisting to 1840*				*Total Persisting to 1840*	*Total Persisting as Per Cent of Original Group*
	I	*II*	*III*	*IV*		
I (128)	25	11	6	1	43	33.6
Per Cent of Persisters	58.1	25.6	14.0	2.3	100.0	
II (60)	5	11	13	2	31	51.6
Per Cent of Persisters	16.1	35.5	41.9	6.5	100.0	
III (50)	1	3	21	9	34	68.0
Per Cent of Persisters	3.1	8.8	61.8	26.5	100.0	
IV (19)	1	–	–	13	14	73.6
Per Cent of Persisters	7.1	–	–	92.9	100.0	
Totals (257)	32	25	40	25	122	47.5
Per Cent of Persisters	26.2	20.5	32.8	20.5	100.0	

Assessment Group[a], 1840, and Number in Group	*Assessment Group in 1850 of Those Persisting to 1850*				*Total Persisting to 1850*	*Total Persisting as Per Cent of Original Group*
	I	*II*	*III*	*IV*		
I (120)	37	7	10	–	54	45.0
Per Cent of Persisters	68.5	13.0	18.5	–	100.0	
II (73)	12	8	12	4	36	49.3
Per Cent of Persisters	33.3	22.2	33.3	11.1	100.0	
III (74)	2	4	33	16	55	74.3
Per Cent of Persisters	3.6	7.3	60.0	29.1	100.0	
IV (21)	–	–	3	15	18	85.7
Per Cent of Persisters	–	–	16.7	83.3	100.0	

Totals (288)	51	19	58	35	163	56.6
Per Cent of Persisters	31.3	11.6	35.6	21.4	100.0	

Assessment Group[a], 1850, and Number in Group	*Assessment Group in 1860 of Those Persisting to 1860*				*Total Persisting to 1860*	*Total Persisting as Per Cent of Original Group*
	I	*II*	*III*	*IV*		
I (143)	41	8	10	–	59	41.3
Per Cent of Persisters	69.5	13.6	16.9	–	100.0	
II (36)	8	5	6	–	19	52.8
Per Cent of Persisters	42.1	26.3	31.6	–	100.0	
III (39)	1	1	8	5	15	38.5
Per Cent of Persisters	6.7	6.7	53.3	33.3	100.0	
IV (31)	–	–	4	15	19	61.3
Per Cent of Persisters	–	–	21.0	79.0	100.0	
Totals (249)	50	14	28	20	112	45.0
Per Cent of Persisters	44.6	12.5	25.0	17.9	100.0	

Mobility Summary by Decades and Total

Change in Assessment Group	*1830-1840*		*1840-1850*		*1850-1860*		*1830-1860 Totals*	
	N	*%*	*N*	*%*	*N*	*%*	*N*	*%*
Upward	42	34.4	49	30.0	29	25.9	120	30.2
None	70	57.4	93	57.1	69	61.6	232	58.4
Downward	10	8.2	21	12.9	14	12.5	45	11.4
Totals	122	100.0	163	100.0	112	100.0	397	100.0

[a]Group I=Property under $200; Group II=Property from $200 to $1000; Group III=Property from $1001 to $10,000; Group IV=Property over $10,000.

Source: Sample data.

bility analysis was done, the records were examined only at ten-year intervals (1830/1840/1850/1860), when five-year intervals would have been better, and biennial or annual intervals best. Accordingly, the records consulted discriminate against the enormous mass of individuals, the most mobile sub-stratum. It seems reasonable to assume that persons of low persistence were also not of the wealthiest classes. The assessment records, then, indicate that there was more "success" than actually occurred, simply because the records were consulted at ten-year intervals, automatically excluding the least "successful," most mobile portion of the population. And, finally, this study has left aside entirely the subjective aspects of mobility—individuals' sense of "getting ahead in the world."

But even among those persons who remained in Boston from 1830 to 1840, from 1840 to 1850, or from 1850 to 1860, "success" came to comparatively few. To admit as many persons as possible to this group, be it recalled, "success" was defined as having been achieved by anyone whose total property assessment increased during the decade following his census sample year. Persons whose total assessment remained static or dropped (with a few exceptions) were deemed "unsuccessful." A few very wealthy individuals, including Elias Hasket Derby, did show assessment decreases, particularly in the 1850's, but this may have been attributable to their having diverted some of their holdings into non-assessable categories such as suburban real estate and other investments. In such cases of assessment decline among the very wealthy, other criteria determined "success," chief among them change of residence to a "better" neighborhood and changes in valuation of personal property.

Generally, if a person remained in Boston as long as ten years during the ante-bellum period, his chances of increasing his property assessment (as distinct from advancing from one assessment group to another) were a little better than even from 1830 to 1850, and about three out of seven in the 1850's. Conversely, the odds were about one in six that his assessment would decrease. From 1830 to 1850, his chances of maintaining the same assess-

Table V-5. Changes, After Ten Years, in Assessments of Sample Members of 1830, 1840, and 1850

Assessment Group[a]	*N*	*Lower Assessment* *N*	*Lower Assessment* *%*	*Same Assessment* *N*	*Same Assessment* *%*	*Higher Assessment* *N*	*Higher Assessment* *%*	*Not Assessed* *N*	*Not Assessed* *%*
					1830 Sample				
I	128	–[b]	–	25	19.5	18	14.1	85	66.4
II	60	7	11.7	4	6.7	20	33.3	29	48.3
III	50	12	24.0	3	6.0	19	38.0	16	32.0
IV	19	4	21.1	–	–	10	52.6	5	26.3
Totals	257	23	9.0	32	12.4	67	26.1	135	52.5
Per Cent of 122 Who Persisted		18.9		26.2		54.9			
					1840 Sample				
I	120	–[b]	–	37	30.8	17	14.2	66	55.0
II	73	13	17.8	1	1.4	22	30.1	37	50.7
III	74	10	13.5	4	5.4	41	55.4	19	25.7
IV	21	4	19.0	–	–	14	66.7	3	14.3
Totals	288	27	9.4	42	14.6	94	32.6	125	43.4
Per Cent of 163 Who Persisted		16.6		25.8		57.7			
					1850 Sample				
I	143	–[b]	–	41	28.7	18	12.6	84	58.1
II	36	10	27.8	2	5.6	7	19.4	17	47.2
III	39	5	12.8	1	2.6	9	23.1	24	61.5
IV	31	5	16.1	–	–	14	45.1	12	38.8
Totals	249	20	8.0	44	17.7	48	19.3	137	55.0
Per Cent of 112 Who Persisted		17.9		39.3		42.8			

[a] I=under $200 (Poll Tax Only); II=$200-$1000; III=$1001-$10,000; IV=over $10,000.

[b] This item is zero since one could not be assessed for less than Poll Tax Only.

Source: Sample data.

Table V-6. Upward and Downward Socioeconomic (Occupational) Mobility of Socioeconomic Group Members, 1830-1860, Compared with Their Persistence

Socio-economic Group (by Number[a]), 1830	*N, 1830*	*Socioeconomic Group (by Number[a]), 1840*									*Total Remaining, 1840*		*Deaths and Out-Migration*	
		1	*2*	*3*	*4*	*5*	*6*	*7*	*8*	*9*	*N*	*%*	*N*	*%*
1	44	12	1	3	1	–	–	–	–	–	17	38.6	27	61.4
2	32	3	8	1	1	–	–	–	–	–	13	40.6	19	59.4
3	64	–	1	18	1	1	–	5	–	3	29	45.3	35	54.7
4	76	1	–	–	26	–	1	–	–	–	28	36.9	48	63.1
5	9	–	–	1	–	2	–	3	–	1	7	77.8	2	22.2
6	7	–	–	–	–	–	2	–	–	–	2	28.6	5	71.4
7	56	–	–	1	–	–	–	27	–	5	33	58.9	23	41.1
8	14	–	–	–	–	–	–	–	8	–	8	42.9	6	57.1
9	83	–	–	–	–	–	–	–	1	25	26	31.3	57	68.7
Totals	385	16	10	24	29	3	3	35	9	34	163	42.4	222	57.6

Socio-economic Group (by Number[a]), 1840	*N, 1840*	*Socioeconomic Group (by Number[a]), 1850*									*Total Remaining, 1850*		*Deaths and Out-Migration*	
		1	*2*	*3*	*4*	*5*	*6*	*7*	*8*	*9*	*N*	*%*	*N*	*%*
1	55	15	1	2	1	1	–	–	–	–	20	36.4	35	63.6
2	24	1	7	–	–	–	1	–	–	–	9	37.5	15	62.5
3	64	–	–	20	–	2	–	2	–	1	25	39.1	39	60.9
4	70	1	1	2	27	–	–	–	–	–	31	44.3	39	55.7
5	8	–	–	–	–	2	–	1	–	–	3	37.5	5	62.5
6	6	–	–	–	–	–	3	–	1	–	4	66.7	2	33.3
7	89	–	–	4	–	–	–	52	–	6	62	69.6	27	30.4
8	8	–	–	–	–	–	–	1	5	–	6	75.0	2	25.0
9	61	1	–	1	1	–	–	–	–	13	16	26.2	45	73.8
Totals	385	18	9	28	29	5	4	56	6	21	176	45.7	209	54.3

Socio-economic Group (by Number[a]), 1850	*N, 1850*	*Socioeconomic Group (by Number[a]), 1860*									*Total Remaining, 1860*		*Deaths and Out-Migration*	
		1	*2*	*3*	*4*	*5*	*6*	*7*	*8*	*9*	*N*	*%*	*N*	*%*
1	104	20	2	4	2	–	–	–	–	1	29	27.9	75	72.1
2	21	–	6	2	1	1	–	–	–	–	10	47.7	11	52.3
3	38	–	3	14	–	1	–	–	–	1	19	50.0	19	50.0
4	98	1	–	–	36	4	–	4	–	–	45	45.9	53	54.1
5	15	–	–	–	–	3	–	1	–	–	4	26.7	11	73.3
6	3	–	–	–	–	–	2	–	–	–	2	66.7	1	33.3
7	44	–	–	–	–	–	–	13	–	3	16	36.4	28	63.6
8	13	–	–	–	–	–	–	–	5	1	6	46.2	7	53.8
9	49	–	–	–	–	–	–	–	–	11	11	22.4	38	77.6
Totals	385	21	11	20	39	9	2	18	5	17	142	36.9	243	63.1

Summary for Those Persisting, by Per Cent

Period	*Number Persisting*	*Retired*	*Higher Group*	*Same Group*		*Lower Group*
				Same Occupation	*Different Occupation*	
1830-1840	100.0	5.5	11.0	74.2	4.3	4.9
(N)	(163)	(9)	(18)	(121)	(7)	(8)
1840-1850	100.0	4.0	6.8	77.8	4.0	7.4
(N)	(176)	(7)	(12)	(137)	(7)	(13)
1850-1860	100.0	4.2	14.8	72.5	4.2	2.8
(N)	(142)	(6)	(21)	(103)	(6)	(4)

[a]1=Unskilled & Menial Service; 2=Semi-Skilled & Service; 3=Petty Proprietors, Managers, & Officials; 4=Skilled; 5=Clerical & Sales; 6=Semi-Professional; 7=Proprietors, Managers, & Officials; 8=Professional; 9=Miscellaneous & Unknown (includes Single Women, Retired Men, and Unknown Occupation).

Source: Sample data.

ment were one in four, rising to two in five for the 1850's. By 1850, the chances of "success," thus measured, were decreasing in Boston (see Table V-5).

Combining all of the heterogeneous data previously presented, one may calculate the chances for individual occupational advancement of members of various socioeconomic groups. These calculations also include deaths and out-migration of group members and thus represent a probability statement for all persons in a given socioeconomic group at the start of each of the three decades.

First, as Table V-6 shows, no socioeconomic group consistently retained a majority of its members in Boston in all three decades. The persistence of three groups declined steadily: Unskilled & Menial, Clerical & Sales, and Miscellaneous & Unknown. In contrast, only the rates of Skilled workers rose throughout. The behavior of other groups was more erratic.

Considering socioeconomic advancement from the point of view solely of rising assessments over ten-year periods, we may summarize in Table V-7 the over-all experiences of the sample members during 1830–60: only one person in five advanced in the 1830's, one in four in the prosperous 'forties, and one in six in the 'fifties. The others fell out along the way.

The question of "success" or advancement, it should be clear by now, depends very much upon how one sets out to measure it. Along a dimension of strict occupational mobility, individuals fared best in the 'fifties, worst in the 'forties, and "in between" during the 'thirties (Table V-6). But gauging "success" in terms of socioeconomic groups indicates that a gap between "higher" and "lower" occupations widened till about 1850, then narrowed. Finally, property assessment groupings (Table V-4) indicate increasing upward *and* downward mobility over the three decades. There is some indication of a relationship between occupational mobility and advancement in assessments, in that during periods of greatest advancement in assessments, such as the 1840's, upward occupational mobility was least and downward greatest, while in the 'fifties upward occupational mobility was highest and

Table V-7. Ultimate Disposition (Death, Out-Migration, Assessment) of Sample Members, 1830-1860 (Per Cent)

Disposition of Sample Members	Sample (N = 385 in Each Case)		
	1830	*1840*	*1850*
Sample at Start of Decade	100.0	100.0	100.0
Known Out-Migrants	9.6	12.5	12.7
Presumed Out-Migrants	29.9[a]	28.1	36.4
Died Outside Boston During Decade (Boston Residents)		0.3	–
Died in Boston During Decade	17.2	13.5	14.0
Remaining in Boston at End of Decade	42.4	45.7	36.9
Not Assessed	10.6	6.0	5.7
Assessed Lower Than at Start of Decade	4.4	5.7	3.6
Assessed Same as at Start of Decade	7.3	10.1	10.9
Assessed More Than at Start of Decade	20.0	23.9	16.6

[a]The two categories were combined for the 1830 sample because statewide death registration did not begin until 1841/1842.

Source: Sample data.

downward lowest, with individual assessment gains the least (*cf.* Tables V-6 and V-7). Perhaps the best conclusion from the information here presented is that "success" is in the eye of the beholder. Writing in 1851, the statistician Jesse Chickering put it well:

> Those who come [to Boston] from other places, bring with them no capital; . . . they come only to gain; . . . the only idea of *success* in their vocabulary, is the acquisition of property; [while] the native population, who are very differently educated, . . . are partly diverted by the attractions and amusements of a city life, . . . so that at length those from abroad gain the control of the business, and of the affairs of their

adopted city. . . . Hence it is that in one generation, the burden of business, and the management of public affairs pass from one set of men to another; . . . .

Of those who resort to cities to better their condition, but a very few *succeed* in obtaining wealth or other reputable distinction. Most of them . . . very soon sink down under the weight of care, labor and misfortune, and perish and are forgotten. The stream continues flowing on to supply the waste. . . . This change is especially to be seen in commercial cities, where . . . the people become migratory, where the succeeding generation is not descended from the preceding by natural affinity, but is gathered together promiscuously and apparently as if by accident, yet overruled by Providence, which leads individuals and communities on to their destination.[16]

VI

Out-Migration from Boston, 1830–1860

The old residents, leaving the low and reclaimed land to foreign laborers, plant themselves in the suburbs. There they build tasteful houses, with flower-plats and gardens; availing [themselves] of the frequent omnibuses, or of special trains run almost hourly, . . . they reach their stores and offices in the morning, and at night sleep with their wives and children in the suburbs. No time is lost, for they read the morning and evening journals as they go and return.

ELIAS H. DERBY[1]

As it is, our mechanics, clerks, and others, are driven to the country to find suitable places at a moderate rent to live in. Deprived of the society of their families, dining at restaurants, and gradually alienated from their domestic hearths, their moral exposure is greater than can be well calculated.

BOSTON SOCIETY FOR THE PREVENTION OF PAUPERISM[2]

Ante-bellum Boston not only served as an attraction to population, but also as a point of departure. The passage of people through cities seems to be one of the more neglected aspects of the entire urbanization process. If Boston, with its approximately 40 per cent interdecadal persistence during 1830–60, was filtering through itself each decade from two to six times as many households as lived in the city at the start of any decade, what of Philadelphia, with its persistence rates of 30 to 38 per cent? What of Rochester's 20 per cent persistence during the 'fifties?[3] It would appear generally that the larger the city, the lower the persistence (during the 1850's) and the more rapid the turnover.[4]

Assuming, for the sake of illustration, that during 1830–60 all American cities over 50,000 displayed residential mobility of 30 per cent per year, half of the population of these cities (as shown in Chapter IV) would have been replaced every two years, or the equivalent of two and one-half times the whole population every decade. Considering this flow, which is about equal to the combined "urban" population of the United States (using a cutoff of 2500) between 1830 and 1860, suggests the possibility that a goodly proportion of America's nineteenth-century "urban" population may have spent some time in a city of over 50,000 (*cf.* Table VI-1). In any event, urbanization was not the "one-way street" we are wont to consider it.

Table VI-1. Comparison of Population in Areas of Over 2500 and of Over 50,000, United States, 1830-1860

	Total Population of All Places Over			
Year	1. *2,500*	2. *50,000*	3. *(2) as Per Cent of (1)*	4. *(3) (Times 2.5 to Estimate Turnover)*
1830	1,127,247	425,063	37.7	94.3
1840	1,845,055	704,264	38.2	95.4
1850	3,543,716	1,459,023	41.2	102.9
1860	6,216,518	3,090,841	49.7	124.3

Source: U.S. Bureau of the Census, *Historical Statistics of the United States Colonial Times to 1957* (Washington: Government Printing Office, 1961), 14.

This chapter essays a description of the fate of Boston's out-migrants, who were, after all, almost as numerous as its immigrants and in-migrants. As nearly as can be determined, no nineteenth-century urban study has dealt with a city's out-migrants. Out-migrants vanish into a historical limbo, gone but not unmourned. One expert declares that "There is . . . no feasible method of tracing individuals once they disappear from the universe of the community under consideration."[5] This attitude has, regrettably, permeated previous urban studies. But there are at least five sources of information on Boston's out-migrants; all have been used in this study.

First, city directories list suburban dwelling places for increasing numbers of Bostonians after about 1850. Second, the records of Boston area cemeteries contain information on the city's residents who wandered away, yet were returned to stay. Third, the Commonwealth of Massachusetts vital statistics records have information, for and after 1841/1842, on births, deaths, and marriages within the state. Any of several events—a person's death, the death of one of his children, his re-marriage, or the marriage of a child—may betray the presence, far from the Hub, of an ex-Bostonian. Fourth, there is the manuscript census itself. For the 1850 and 1860 federal censuses, which alone during the study period permit positive identification of individuals by comparison of given names, one has but to search the lists of residents in areas surrounding the study area. With practice, millions of names may be screened. For instance, in the present study, in addition to Boston the manuscript census lists (on microfilm) of 128 other Massachusetts cities and towns were checked. And last, genealogies and town histories often mentioned out-migrants' destinations.

Of the sample members in 1830, 1840, and 1850, from 15 to 18 per cent died in the subsequent decade. Another 9.1 to 12.7 per cent were positively identified as out-migrants, while from 36 to 45 per cent remained in Boston at the end of each decade. Between 28 and 36 per cent of each sample could not be accounted for at decade's end, and was presumed to have left Boston (and probably Massachusetts). If one assumes the death rate among those not accounted for was about the same as that among those who remained (15–18 per cent), the proportion of living unknowns at decade's end would drop to about 30 per cent. Since the state registration was fairly efficient, one may conclude they had left the state. Until the manuscript census returns for the entire United States are data-processed, these persons must be considered lost. Nevertheless, we may still compare the pre-departure records of the "lost" 30 per cent with those of persons who stayed, thus characterizing some of the qualities of "transients" as against those of "continuous residents."

The general characteristics of those who left Boston were not, in most cases, markedly different from those of persons persisting in the city. The relative socioeconomic status group distributions, for example (Table VI-2), manifested distinct differences only among the Proprietors, Managers, & Officials and Unskilled & Menial Service categories. Up to 1850, the former was under-represented among out-migrants, while after 1840 the latter was over-represented.

Dividing the samples into assessment groups (as in Chapter V) produces similar results. As one might expect, non-assessed males showed a marked tendency to leave Boston. But among those who paid only a poll tax, no especially wide gap opened between transients and "persisters" until the 1850's, when a greater proportion of "poll-tax-only" payers remained in Boston, reversing the previous trend (see Table VI-3). Persons with only a small amount of property ($200–$1000) were about one and one-fifth to two times as likely to remain in Boston as to leave, as Table VI-4 demonstrates. An anomaly crops up among the "upper middle" group ($1001–$10,000), though. During the 1830's, persons in this group were almost twice as likely to remain as to leave; the margin opened to three to one during the 'forties, only to reverse in the 'fifties to about three-quarters to one, indicating a substantial out-migration among this group. George Adams, who took the 1850 state census of Boston, may have had this "upper middle" group in mind when he wrote that

> many, especially for the last ten years, doing business in Boston, had become residents of the neighboring towns. These removals have not only been numerous, but many who have entered the City for the purpose of engaging in business have retained their country residences. The multiplied conveniences of travelling have in part induced to this. . . .
>
> The Boston Directory contains the names of nearly 4000 persons doing business in Boston, and residing out of town. . . . it has been estimated that the whole number of individuals

Table VI-2. Socioeconomic Status Group Composition of Persisting and Out-Migrating Sample Members, 1830-1860, by Per Cent

Socioeconomic Status Group	*Sample and Per Cent*								
	1830			*1840*			*1850*		
	Persisting	*Out-Migrating*	*Total Sample*	*Persisting*	*Out-Migrating*	*Total Sample*	*Persisting*	*Out-Migrating*	*Total Sample*
Unskilled & Menial Service	10.5	11.2	11.4	11.4	20.5	14.3	20.4	33.3	27.0
Semi-Skilled & Service	8.0	8.6	8.3	5.1	6.4	6.2	7.0	4.8	5.5
Petty Proprietors, Managers, & Officials	17.8	15.2	16.9	14.2	17.9	16.6	13.4	7.4	9.9
Skilled	17.2	21.8	19.7	17.6	18.6	18.2	31.7	23.3	25.4
Clerical & Sales	4.3	0.7	2.3	1.7	1.3	2.1	2.8	3.7	3.9
Semi-Professional	1.3	2.7	1.8	2.3	0.6	1.6	1.4	—	0.8
Proprietors, Managers, & Officials	20.3	13.9	14.5	35.2	10.9	23.1	11.3	12.2	11.4
Professional	4.9	2.7	3.6	3.4	0.6	2.1	4.2	2.6	3.4
Miscellaneous & Unknown	16.0	23.7	21.3	9.1	23.1	15.8	7.7	12.7	12.7
Total in Sample	163	152	385	183	148	385	142	189	385

Because some sample members died, the sum of "persisting" and "out-migrating" sample members does not equal 385.
Source: Sample data.

Table VI-3. Assessment Group Composition of Persisting and Out-Migrating Sample Members, 1830-1860, by Per Cent

		Assessment Group					
Sample and Characteristic	*N*	*Not Assessed Male*	*Not Assessed Female*	*Under $200*	*$200- $1,000*	*$1,001- $10,000*	*Over $10,000*
1830							
Persisting	163	9.2	16.6	28.8	19.0	18.4	8.0
Out-Migrating	152	22.4	17.1	32.9	14.5	11.2	2.0
Total Sample	385	15.6	17.2	33.3	16.1	13.0	4.9
1840							
Persisting	176	5.1	8.0	30.7	19.3	27.8	9.1
Out-Migrating	156	23.7	15.4	33.3	17.3	9.0	1.3
Total Sample	385	13.2	11.9	31.2	19.0	19.2	5.5
1850							
Persisting	142	16.2	7.0	45.8	12.0	7.7	11.3
Out-Migrating	189	33.3	12.7	32.8	6.9	10.1	4.2
Total Sample	385	25.2	10.1	37.1	9.4	10.1	8.1

Because some sample members died, the sum of "persisting" and "out-migrating" sample members does not equal 385.

Source: Sample data.

doing business in Boston, and residing in the country, including their families, would amount to 20,000.[6]

It is unlikely that Adams referred to the very rich (assessed over $10,000), for as Table VI-4 shows, up to 1850 these persons were two or three times as likely to stay in Boston as to leave it. Together, Tables VI-2, VI-3, and VI-4 indicate that the persons most likely to leave Boston were (after 1840) generally propertyless unskilled individuals. Those most likely to remain were (up till 1850) the major managers, proprietors, and officials worth more than $1000. After 1850, though, there occurred a considerable departure of this class, forming a noticeable fraction of Boston's outward-flowing population.

Table VI-4. Persistence Rates of Members of Various Assessment Groups, 1830-1860

Sample and Characteristic	N	Assessment Group: Not Assessed Male	Not Assessed Female	Under $200	$200-$1,000	$1,001-$10,000	Over $10,000
1830							
Present in 1830	385	60	66	127	62	50	19
Present in 1840	163	15	27	47	31	30	13
Persistence Rate (Per Cent)	42.4	25.0	40.9	37.0	50.0	60.0	68.4
1840							
Present in 1840	385	51	46	120	73	74	21
Present in 1850	176	9	14	54	34	49	16
Persistence Rate (Per Cent)	45.7	17.6	30.4	45.0	46.6	66.2	76.2
1850							
Present in 1850	385	97	39	143	36	39	31
Present in 1860	142	23	10	65	17	11	16
Persistence Rate (Per Cent)	36.9	23.7	25.6	45.5	47.2	28.2	51.6

Sample	Total of All Assessed: Present in Sample Year	Present After Ten Years	Persistence Rate (Per Cent)
1830	257	122	47.5
1840	288	163	56.6
1850	249	112	45.0

Source: Sample data.

Before examining the out-migration patterns revealed by the sample groups, it may be that census data can illuminate the situation somewhat. We are of course handicapped in that antebellum censuses taken in Massachusetts never inquired where persons had lived previously. But in 1850 and 1860 the federal census, and in 1855 the state census, contained nativity questions.

This permits a gross separation of population into native-born and foreign-born. Irish predominated in the latter (about 75 per cent). It was these foreign-born individuals whose exceptional mobility into, within, and out of Boston formed such a striking feature of Chapter IV. Because of their visibility in the census returns, and because their residential mobility formed such a large portion of Boston's residential mobility, their distribution should show some of the major characteristics of the outflowing population of Boston. This presumes that most Irish who lived in Massachusetts had been "processed" through Boston, and that backflow from New York City (the nearest other major port of entry) was negligible. The first seems likely, given Boston's position as a railroad center after 1845. The second assumption would appear reasonable since interstate migration statistics for native-born individuals show little backflow from New York to Massachusetts.[7]

The 1855 state census provides the period's only town-by-town breakdown of nativity figures; its major results appear in Table VI-5 (in this census, "foreign-born" did not include native-born children of foreign parents). It shows the marked clustering of foreign-born around Boston. In 1855, some 25.7 per cent of the state's native-born residents lived within ten miles of Boston, as against 44.3 per cent of the foreign-born. The foreign-born were progressively less prevalent farther from Boston, with one foreigner out of four in Massachusetts living in Boston itself, one out of eight in the contiguous cities and towns, and one out of sixteen in the rest of the towns to a distance of ten miles from Boston. Perhaps a good place to look for Boston's out-migrants, or at least quite a few of them, would be in the suburban cities and towns to a distance of ten miles.

Of the 1155 sample members of the 1830, 1840, and 1850 samples, 37, 48, and 49, respectively, were definitely identified as out-migrants by being located in a census outside Boston after their disappearance from Boston. These 134 persons represent just over 11 per cent of the 1155, and account for only 27 per cent of the 497 out-migrants during 1830–60 (i.e., 134 "known" and 363 "presumed"). Table VI-6 compares the socioeconomic status

Table VI-5. Distribution of Total and Foreign-Born Population in Boston and Nearby Areas, 1855

Area	1. *Total Population in the Area*	2. *Foreign-Born*[a] *Population in the Area*	3. *(2) as Per Cent of (1)*	4. *(1) as Per Cent of State Population*	5. *(2) as Per Cent of Total Foreign-Born in State*	6. *[(1)-(2)] as Per Cent of Native-Born in State*
Boston	160,490	62,353	38.9	14.2	25.4	11.1
Contiguous Cities and Towns	97,411	29,532	30.3	8.8	12.0	7.7
All Other Cities and Towns Within Ten Miles of Boston	77,583	16,823	21.7	7.0	6.9	6.9

[a]Foreign-born does not include native-born children of foreign parents.

Source: Massachusetts. Secretary of the Commonwealth, *Abstract of the Census of the Commonwealth of Massachusetts . . . 1855 . . .* (Boston: William White, 1857), 105-7, 115-21, 123, 126, 132.

Table VI-6. Socioeconomic Status Group and Assessment Group of Known and Assumed Out-Migrants, 1830-1860, by Per Cent

	Sample and Per Cent					
	1830		*1840*		*1850*	
Socioeconomic Status Group	*Known/Assumed Out-Migrants*		*Known/Assumed Out-Migrants*		*Known/Assumed Out-Migrants*	
Unskilled & Menial Service	8.1	12.2	8.3	25.9	2.0	44.3
Semi-Skilled & Service	2.7	10.5	2.1	8.3	6.1	4.3
Petty Proprietors, Managers, & Officials	24.4	12.2	27.1	13.9	8.2	7.1
Skilled	21.7	21.8	22.9	16.7	22.4	23.6
Clerical & Sales	–	0.9	2.1	0.9	10.2	1.4
Semi-Professional	2.7	2.6	–	0.9	–	–
Proprietors, Managers, & Officials	32.5	7.9	25.0	4.6	38.8	2.9
Professional	2.7	2.6	–	0.9	6.1	1.4
Miscellaneous & Unknown	5.4	29.6	12.5	27.8	6.1	15.0
Assessment Group						
Not Assessed–Males	5.4	27.9	6.3	31.5	6.1	42.9
Not Assessed–Females	5.4	20.0	8.3	18.5	6.1	15.0
Under $200	29.8	34.0	33.3	33.3	36.7	31.4
$200-$1,000	27.1	10.5	27.1	13.0	8.2	6.4
$1,001-$10,000	21.7	7.9	20.8	3.7	28.6	3.6
Over $10,000	10.9	–	4.2	–	14.3	0.7
Totals (N)	37	115	48	108	49	140

Source: Sample data.

group and assessment group characteristics of the 134 known and 363 presumed out-migrants. Generally, the out-migrants who were tracked down in censuses outside Boston tended to belong to the Petty Proprietors, Managers, & Officials, the Skilled, and the Proprietors, Managers, & Officials socioeconomic status groups and (until 1850) to cluster in the Under $200 and $200–$1000 assessment categories. After 1850, there occurred a sharp shift toward the wealthier tax brackets of $1001 and above.

Although the 134 known out-migrants represented a generally better off, more elevated socioeconomic group than did the 363 presumed out-migrants, nonetheless it should be interesting to glance briefly at the smaller group, since it does constitute the only considerable number of urban out-migrants ever located.

Geographically, the known out-migrants tended to settle near Boston; more than half of those located had moved less than ten miles from Boston's Merchants' Exchange. Table VI-7 suggests

Table VI-7. Distances from Boston's Merchants' Exchange at Which Known Out-Migrants Settled, 1830-1860

	Sample					
Number of Miles from Exchange at Which Residing	*1830 Known Out-Migrants in 1840*		*1840 Known Out-Migrants in 1850*		*1850 Known Out-Migrants in 1860*	
	Number	*Per Cent*	*Number*	*Per Cent*	*Number*	*Per Cent*
1-5	13	35.1	22	45.8	23	46.9
6-10	7	18.9	10	20.8	13	26.5
11-49	7	18.9	10	20.8	11	22.4
50 and over	5	13.5	6	12.5	2	4.1
Unknown[a]	5	13.5	–	–	–	–
Totals	37	99.9	48	99.9	49	99.9

[a]Distance was deemed "unknown" when individual was known, by death record, to have died outside Boston, yet could not be located in the town of demise in a preceding census; because of frequency of "stage" migration, such persons might have moved to another town from Boston, and then to the town of demise.

Source: Sample data.

that, after the 1840's (when census identification became easier), the proportion of known out-migrants who had moved less than ten miles from Boston rose to about three-quarters. It was during the late 'forties that *commutation* became widespread in Boston; as distinct from the former home-to-work journey, commutation required conveyances. Of course, well-to-do individuals had for some time used their carriages to travel from, say, suburban Roxbury or Brighton into the business section of Boston. (As early as 1846, complaints appeared in a Boston newspaper about persons who tied down the reins of their carriages but did not hitch the reins to streetside posts; this allowed horse and carriage gradually to wander along a street, blocking traffic.[8])

The phenomenon of population dispersion to the suburbs did not escape contemporaries. One of the first to comment on the process was Jesse Chickering:

> In consequence of traveling facilities by railroads radiating in every direction from Boston, as a common centre; many merchants and others doing business in the City, have of late been induced to remove to the neighboring towns whence they can go to the places of their daily business as quickly and as cheaply as if they had continued in their former residences.[9]

By 1852, the City Council's Committee on Public Lands noted that

> A reference to the census will show that while our foreign population is rapidly augmenting, our native population is in a greater ratio diminishing. The great influx of foreigners is changing entirely the character of various portions of the City. . . .
>
> The older parts of the City are crowded, rents are exorbitant, and it is with extreme difficulty that a comfortable tenement can be obtained.
>
> Many citizens of Boston are erecting houses in the neighboring cities and villages, and increasing the taxable property in those places from the profits of business transacted within our limits. . . .
>
> The Committee are of opinion that the true interest of the City requires that every proper inducement should be offered to incline our citizens to remain within our limits.[10]

And that, of course, was the experience of the more prosperous Bostonians, for a student of Boston's ante-bellum commutation system has described a dichotomy operating in the outward spread of the city's population. The cost of commutation was beyond the means of the ordinary laborer. Thus Boston's population divided into at least three groups: persons remaining in the city, persons commuting from the suburbs, and persons who moved to the suburbs but could not afford to commute.[11] In substantiation of these findings, we have noticed that after 1840 propertyless unskilled individuals contributed heavily to the outward movement. After 1850 there was a considerable admixture of the "upper-middle" commuters whose principal real property in Boston had consisted of their homes, with the bulk of their holdings in "personal estate" at their business locations. It was thus easier for them to remove from the city than it was for persons with extensive real estate holdings; these, the "upper class," tended to remain in Boston.

A prominent feature of previous studies on population mobility has been the assumption that persons who left an area were doing so, among other reasons, because they were not as "successful" as their contemporaries. As far as ante-bellum Boston is concerned, this assumption appears plausible, for, generally, prior economic achievement was a good predictor of persistence in Boston. The fact that the 1850 and 1860 federal censuses contained wealth questions means that persons who left Boston may be compared, as to wealth, with those who remained. The results of such comparisons are presented with some diffidence, for though individuals who refused to "render a true account . . . in the various particulars required in and by" the census act of 1850 might be fined $30, about one household head in 14 lied about his real estate holdings, or omitted to mention them, or was victimized by a clerical omission of their amount (see Table VI-8).[12] This illustrates the dangers of using any wealth figures derived from the manuscript census alone.[13]

Persons who were assessed in Boston in 1850 (as 1850 sample

Table VI-8. Real Estate Assessments, 1850, of Persons Listed in the Federal Manuscript Census as Owning No Real Estate

Assessment Category	*Number in Category*	*As Per Cent of Total Sample (385)*
Not Assessed—Male	99	25.7
Not Assessed—Female	39	10.1
Poll Tax Only (Under $200 in Property)	140	36.4
Assessed for Some Personal Property but no Real Estate	42	10.9
(Total Not Assessed for Real Estate)	(320)	(83.1)
$301-$500[a]	4	1.0
$501-$1,000	6	1.6
$1,501-$2,500[a]	6	1.6
$2,501-$5,000	4	1.0
$5,001-$10,000	4	1.0
$10,001-$25,000[a]	4	1.0
(Total Assessed for Real Estate But Not Listed in Census as Owning Real Estate)	(28)	(7.3)
(Total Assessed for Real Estate and Listed in Census as Owning Real Estate)	(37)	(9.6)
Totals	385	100.0

[a]The assessment categories $200-$300, $1,001-$1,500, and $25,001 and over were omitted because their entries were zero.

Source: Sample data.

members) and who were again assessed in 1860, together with a few others whose assessment could be deduced although it was not available, numbered 142 (deducing the assessments of 30 additional persons introduces a slight discrepancy from the re-

Table VI-9. Comparison of Changes in Assessment Group, 1850-1860, of 142 "Persisters" and 31 Known Out-Migrants

"PERSISTERS"

Assessment Group, 1850	*N*	*Number in Assessment Groups, 1860*				*Change*	*Number*	*Per Cent*
		I	*II*	*III*	*IV*			
I (Under $200)	98	74	10	13	1			
II ($200-$1000)	17	8	4	5	—	Upward	32	22.5
						None	94	66.2
III ($1001-$10,000)	11	2	1	5	3	Downward	16	11.3
						Totals	142	100.0
IV (Over $10,000)	16	1	—	4	11			
Totals	142	85	15	27	15			

KNOWN OUT-MIGRANTS

Assessment Group, 1850	*N*	*Numbers in Wealth Categories Corresponding to Assessment Groups, as Listed in the 1860 Manuscript Census*				*Change*	*Number*	*Per Cent*
		I	*II*	*III*	*IV*			
I (Under $200)	16	9	2	5	—			
II ($200-$1000)	2	—	—	2	—	Upward	13	41.9
						None	15	48.4
III ($1001-$10,000)	9	1	—	4	4	Downward	3	9.7
						Totals	31	100.0
IV (Over $10,000)	4	1	—	1	2			
Totals	31	11	2	12	6			

Source: Sample data.

sults in Table V-4). Of these, by 1860 about one in five had advanced to a higher assessment group (as defined in Chapter V). About two-thirds remained in the same group, and approximately one-ninth had slipped to a lower group. However, of the 31 persons known to have left Boston in the 1850's for whom 1860 census reports were found, more than two-fifths had moved to the equivalent of a higher assessment group. Nearly half were still in the same bracket, and only one-tenth had dropped to a lower category (see Table VI-9). Since the known out-migrants were better off in 1850 than were the "persisters," the former would be expected to have enjoyed surperior opportunities for advancement. Nevertheless, when we compare the performance of the propertyless individuals in each group, we note that of the 98 "persisters" only 24 (24.5 per cent) had obtained property as of 1860. But of the 16 propertyless (as of 1850) who became known out-migrants, 7 (43.8 per cent) owned some property by 1860, suggesting that about twice as many of them had become property-owners of some sort.

These fragmentary data should suffice to indicate that the little-known portion of the urbanization process occurring *after* arrival at a population center is the part currently subject to the most facile (and perhaps least accurate) generalizations. These generalizations, which concern the relationship of "success" and persistence, have yet to be examined rigorously. The requisite examination would seem, unfortunately, to be beyond the resources of individuals using current methods. Yet the data here presented argue that this very area of concern—which might be called the "post-urban" part of the urbanization process—is not only of great intrinsic importance, but has also been allowed to languish untilled, its boundaries and characteristics those of a *terra incognita*.

VII

Summing Up and Looking Ahead

> If sufficient data were recovered or reconstructed, the urbanization of population could be correlated with structural characteristics of an economic or social kind, their associations analyzed, and clothed in all the rich detail of historicity.
>
> ERIC E. LAMPARD[1]

This study began with a number of apparently simple questions one might have assumed amenable to unequivocal responses. The questions included: where did the population of Boston, 1830–60, come from? What did the city's people do for a living? How well did they do? Where did they live, and for how long? Where did they go when they left? The inquiries were conceived in a spirit which determinedly distanced itself from hypotheses and models of population behavior, proceeding from the empirical premise that facts must precede theories.

In this light, the study's principal historical conclusion must be that there are more unexplored aspects of the urbanization process than were previously dreamt of in our philosophy. Every question here illuminated has spawned subsidiary questions to puzzle others who would venture to study urban history. Samuel Johnson defined a *network* as "any thing reticulated . . . , with interstices between the intersections"; this study should make the reader—as it has the writer—uncomfortably aware of the preponderance of interstices over intersections in the network of our knowledge of urbanization. We cast a great net, but its meshes are also large. A review of some intersections, as well as an indication of some interstices—foci of future studies!—is in order.

The sources of Boston's population changed during the ante-bellum era. Until the 1840's the city's growth was dominated demographically by native-born persons who hailed usually from small agricultural towns in northern New England. These persons moved to Boston, remained there perhaps fifteen years, and moved on. One may conjecture that a larger proportion of them returned to their hometowns than was later the case, for in checking the early state death records (up to about 1850), one sees that many persons who died were returned to small upcountry towns for interment. But after about 1850, there seems to have occurred a loosening of bonds to the old hometown, for the trend shifted toward metropolitan interment in the new "garden cemeteries." *

During the mid-1840's the influx of Irish and other foreigners began. The large number of unskilled workers among the Irish seems to have depressed the market for unskilled labor so much that many unskilled native-born workers left Boston. This outflow of native-born was reflected in the composition, by nativity, of Boston's population over the decade following 1845 (see Table VII-1). By 1855 the city of Puritan fathers was well on its way toward the Irish-American political dominance which has characterized it since the 1870's.

With the large influx of unskilled and mostly illiterate foreigners, there came as well a pervasive change in Boston's occupational structure or labor force profile. The day of the skilled worker as the linchpin of society—the fabled "industrious mechanic"—passed quickly in ante-bellum Boston. By 1850 over half the work force was unskilled or semi-skilled, much of it dependent upon day-to-day casual labor. Here was a large labor pool that might have fostered the growth in the city of extensive manufacturing estab-

* This conjecture is subject to statistical verification. Few students have examined the questions of cemeteries' position and functions in 19th-century America. The records of at least one of the early garden cemeteries, Woodlawn in Everett, are available, at the Woodlawn Cemetery's office. Certainly there was gross class discrimination by cemeteries of their patrons.

Table VII-1. Nativity of Boston's Population, 1845-1855

		Per Cent	
Year	*Total Population*	*Native-Born*	*Foreign-Born*[a]
1845	114,366	67.4	32.6
1850	138,788	54.3	45.7
1855	161,429	47.0	53.0

[a]Foreign-born includes native-born children with foreign parents (whether one or both was foreign is not stated).

Source: Report of the Joint Special Committee on the Census of Boston, May, 1855. . . . (Boston: Moore & Crosby, 1856), 21.

lishments employing many unskilled hands. But the very heaping of many unskilled workers at the center of the city helped drive up rents there, encouraging a shift of large-scale manufacturing toward peripheral and suburban locations. Table VII-2 suggests the extent of this outward movement during the 1850's; it involved an over-all loss of about half the city's manufacturing establishments, as well as a 40 per cent drop in the number of "hands" in the central area of the city. Doubtless there were also effects of a change in the *scale* of manufacturing operations. Even with the decline in the number of hands employed in the central wards, their average product rose from $1066 in 1850 to $1680 in 1860, while corresponding figures for peripheral workers were $1643 and $2383, and for the whole city $1196 and $1928. Detailed analysis of the census manufacturing schedules would probably clarify this question.

Movement, mobility, shifts, change—these words can suggest only faintly the extent and pervasiveness of what occurred among Boston's people during the ante-bellum era. In each of the three decades at least two to six times as many families passed through the city as lived in it at the start of any decade. The native-born, coming mostly from small towns in upper New England, formed the most stable part of the population: on the average, they moved around the city less frequently, and stayed longer, than did the

Table VII-2. Statistics of Manufacturing, Boston, 1850 and 1860

Characteristic and Area	*1850*	*1860*	*Change, 1850-1860 (Per Cent)*
Number of Establishments			
Central Wards	1208	713	− 41.0
Peripheral Wards	706	289	− 59.1
City	1914	1002	− 47.6
Number of Hands Employed			
Central Wards	20,424	12,101	− 40.8
Peripheral Wards	5,897	6,625	+ 12.3
City	26,321	18,726	− 28.9
Average Number of Hands per Establishment			
Central Wards	16.91	16.96	+ 0.03
Peripheral Wards	8.35	22.94	+174.7
City	13.75	18.69	+ 35.9
Total Product (Current Dollars)			
Central Wards	$21,782,870	$20,321,593	− 6.7
Peripheral Wards	9,688,406	15,788,232	+ 63.0
City	$31,471,276	$36,109,825	+ 14.7
Average Product per Establishment (Current Dollars)			
Central Wards	$18,032	$28,502	+ 58.1
Peripheral Wards	13,723	54,631	+298.1
City	$16,443	$36,038	+119.2

Sources: U.S. Census (1850), Schedule 5 (Products of Industry), Boston (microfilm from Massachusetts Archives); U.S. Census Office. Eighth Census (1860), *Manufactures of the United States in 1860 . . .* (Washington: Government Printing Office, 1865), 248.

foreign-born. Despite the accelerating urbanization of New England during the ante-bellum period, in-migrants from upcountry continued throughout the period to come primarily from small towns rather than large towns; very few came from cities. Once arrived in Boston, the native-born favored the peripheral areas, while the foreign-born tended to cluster at the city's center. As the proportion of foreign-born in the population rose, the rate of residential mobility increased, quickening the "churning" of the city's people.

The arrival of large numbers of foreigners coincided also with changes in patterns of "success" in Boston. During the 'forties, individuals did best as far as advancement in monetary terms was concerned, but worst where upward mobility in jobs was concerned.

Table VII-3. Average Assessments, 1830-1860, of Sample Members and of All Taxpayers

	Average Assessment (Current Dollars)			
Group	*1830*	*1840*	*1850*	*1860*
All Taxed Sample Members	$3450	$3275	$ 3950	$10680
All Sample Members Owning Property	6875	5620	9210	24470
All Taxpayers (including Business Firms)	4515	4940	5540	6695
All Taxpayers Owning Property (including Business Firms)	8140	9095	13025	15690

Source: Sample data.

The 'thirties displayed "medium" upward occupational mobility, combined with "medium" economic advance. The 'fifties showed two extremes: high upward occupational mobility but low economic gains, as measured by tax assessments. Meanwhile, wealth in Boston was becoming concentrated in relatively ever fewer hands. As Table VII-3 shows, between 1830 and 1860, the average tax assessment (in current dollars) of all taxpayers rose almost 50 per cent, if undifferentiated totals are used. The sample data, however, correct the undifferentiated totals by eliminating assessments of business firms. When individuals only are considered, the average assessment of propertied persons almost quadruples over the 30 years. Yet at the same time, the proportion of propertyless taxpayers rose from 44.6 per cent in 1830, through 45.7

per cent in 1840, to 57.5 per cent in 1850 and 57.3 per cent in 1860, as the assessment records show. More wealth was in fewer hands.

Certainly this uneven distribution of wealth could have contributed to persons' leaving Boston. The fact remains that there were few differences between the wealth distribution, at the beginning of each decade, of persons who left Boston during the decade and of persons who stayed till the end of the decade. When out-migrants from Boston were pursued to their suburban retreats, they proved on the whole to have done better during the 'fifties than did the general population persisting in Boston. But since these out-migrants were usually better off to start with, the finding is not surprising. Considering propertyless out-migrants, though, we note that generally during the 'fifties they outperformed propertyless persons who stayed in the city.

Among the less specific results of this study has been the demonstration that manuscript and published census data are obviously inadequate to detect many phenomena occurring among populations. Thus, studies of urbanization must use census information as a *terminus a quo* from which to proceed. Every other kind of information which can provide data about large numbers of people should be called to use.

Of course, the very diversity of the kinds of records available, the fact that they are often scattered, that they were collected for purposes other than the researcher's—all this militates against his fashioning a coherent picture of urban events and processes. It may be unpleasant to contemplate, but we ought not to dismiss the possibility that some urban processes of the nineteenth century may ultimately reduce to chaos. That is, at least, they may not be susceptible of reduction to a relatively precise prose description. Such possibilities suggest themselves most strongly when one considers the continuous shuffling of individuals, families, and firms that occurred in ante-bellum Boston. A possible reason for a large part of this redistribution may have been the city's inadequate communications network. Lack of information that other firms were moving to another area, for instance, may explain the frequently observed phenomenon of one firm's shifting diametrically away from the direction taken by most other firms in a given specialty. Because face-to-face contact was necessary for the transaction of most business, one wonders whether firms that moved away from the direction favored by others suffered as a result. This would suggest the need for rather detailed considerations not only of the spatial arrangement of population—as in this study—but also of the distribution of business and industry within cities. Best would be a combination of both. This might illuminate some of the apparently aimless or contradictory movements of persons and businesses.

Similarly, this study has identified as a crucial period in Boston's history the decade of the 1840's. That is, if one had to choose among the three ante-bellum decades that which would be most informative demographically, socially, and economically, he would be well advised to pick the middle decade. Almost every measure gathered for this study changed sharply during the 'forties. In most cases the events of the 'fifties were merely continuations or intensifications of those of the 'forties.

All that has gone before should suggest that the process of urbanization deserves much closer study than it has had. The "process" of urbanization, in fact, might better be called the "cycle" of urbanization, for one of this study's major findings is that, during the ante-bellum era, residence in a city occupied only a part of many individual's lives. In asking how urbanization affected people, we tend to assume that it was a one-way experience, with people accumulating in population centers. This was not so: there was considerable population flow *through* Boston to destinations largely unknown to us. Here there is an opportunity for a major study of the urbanization "cycle" which would catch people before they moved to the city and examine them in their native environment, then look at their performance in the city. It would conclude by checking up on them after they had left the study city. There would appear to be, incidentally, no reason why such a study could not use manuscript census data from at least Great Britain and Ireland, which would account for a majority of immigrants in many areas.[2] The greatest stumbling-block would be that of matching individuals from one source to another. But advancing technology will eventually dissolve this impediment. Then we would have the ideal—studies of individuals before, during, and after exposure to the urban environment. It would be possible as well to select two control groups along the way, persons who stay in rural areas, and rural-born persons who move to cities and stay. Study of their characteristics could not fail to contribute mightily to our knowledge, for instance, of "urban-rural differences," much discussed but poorly specified. In subsequent studies I hope to address some of these questions, particularly with regard to the internal migration process, on which research is already under way.

Appendix A

Using City Directories in Ante-Bellum Urban Historical Research*

With the recent republication on microfiche[1] of the city directories listed in Dorothea N. Spear's *Bibliography of American Directories Through 1860,*[2] and with the intention of the republisher to continue the directory republication project (on microfilm—a vast improvement) into the post-bellum era, it is safe to predict an increase in the use of city directories as urban studies source materials. But there seems to have been no attempt to gauge the inclusivity (or coverage) of these directories, in order to allow for their omissions in using them as information sources about city populations.[3] This Appendix will present some information and data derived from study of Boston's directories during the 1830–60 period. It will also provide some suggestions and warnings to users of ante-bellum directories; only time will tell whether the information here presented has more than parochial application, but it may serve others as a point of departure.[4]

City directories came into existence at various times in different cities during the ante-bellum era. To allow for fly-by-night and irregular directory publication, an arbitrary standard has been selected for the present study: if a city attained the level of supporting the publication of seven directories in ten consecutive

* This Appendix, in a slightly different version, appeared in *Historical Methods Newsletter* 2 (Sept. 1969), 1–10.

years, it was considered that "sustained" directory publication had been achieved. No city studied receded from that level thereafter. Applying this criterion leads to the conclusion that there was a strong relationship between size of place and commencement of "sustained" directory publication (see Table A-1). City sizes in the year of achieving "sustained" directory publication ranged from an estimated 3900 (Fitchburg, Mass., 1846) to New Orleans' estimated 105,000 the same year. Of the thirty cities in Table A-1, twenty were among the nation's thirty largest as of 1850. The rank-order correlation (Spearman rho) between

Table A-1. Number and Average Population of Cities Attaining "Sustained" (Seven Years in Ten) City Directory Publication, by Decade, 1786-1854

Decade	*Number of Cities Attaining "Sustained" (Seven Years in Ten) City Directory Publication*	*Average Population (in Thousands) of Cities at Time of Attaining "Sustained" Directory Publication*[a]
1786-1795	2	26.6
1796-1805	1	29.6
1806-1815	2	22.9
1816-1825	1	8.4
1826-1835	4	10.8
1836-1845	8	17.7
1846-1854[b]	12	26.8[c, d] 19.0[e]
Total	30[c]	21.2[c]

[a]Populations were estimated for intercensal years by logarithmic interpolation.
[b]Since the definition of "sustained" publication calls for knowledge of publication of seven directories in ten successive years, compilation must stop six years before the end point of the Spear bibliography.
[c]Includes New Orleans.
[d]The population of New Orleans in 1840 was taken as 90,000, making its estimated 1846 population 105,000.
[e]Excludes New Orleans.

Sources: Dorothea N. Spear, comp., *Bibliography of American Directories Through 1860* (Worcester, Mass.: American Antiquarian Society, 1961), *passim.*; U.S. Census Office. Twelfth Census (1900), *Census Reports Volume I . . . Population Part I . . .* (Washington: U.S. Census Office, 1901), 430-33.

population in 1850 and order of reaching "sustained" directory publication was +0.84 for the twenty largest cities ($P < 0.01$).

Perhaps a more comprehensive way to observe the rapid spread of directory publication in the ante-bellum era is to sum the total population of areas having directories and to compare the total with that of other population components. From 1790 to 1860, for instance, the nation's population rose from 3.9 to 31.4 million, or 701 per cent. But the total of persons living in places of over 2500 population (the modern urban definition) went from 202,000 to 6.2 million, an advance of 2980 per cent. Great as this relative gain was, it was overshadowed by that of the area covered by city directories (excluding business directories). In 1790, directories served areas inhabited by 67,528 persons; by 1860, the coverage area held 5,011,693—a jump of 7320 per cent. Table A-2 compares the sizes of the three population components and their rates of increase for 1790–1860.

Not all of the directories were *city* directories; by 1860, some hundreds of thousands of persons in rural (using the 2500-person breakpoint) areas also were listed. For example, directories covered Henry County, Iowa (18,701 residents in 1860), and Kane County, Illinois (population of 30,062 in 1860), by 1860. But central cities constituted the vast bulk of the population covered by directories.

Boston had directories for 1790, 1800, and 1810, but did not satisfy the criterion of "sustained" directory publication—seven directories in ten years—until as late as 1813, as did Albany. Boston's population was then about 36,500, Albany's 9300. They were the fourth and fifth cities to qualify, following New York (1786: 23,600), Philadelphia (1791: 29,600), and Baltimore (1802: 29,600).

Boston's ante-bellum city directories were published between 1820 and 1846 by Charles Stimpson (a stationer and bookseller born in Virginia to Massachusetts parents), apparently as a sideline to his business. In 1846 there appeared a competing directory under the name of George Adams, one of America's first professional canvassers, who advertised himself as an agent,

Table A-2. Populations of Areas Covered by Directories, Compared with Those of All "Urban" (over 2500) Places and of the United States, with Per Cent Decadal Growth Rates, 1790-1860

Year	*Population in Areas Covered by Directories (Thousands)*	*Per Cent Change in Decade*	*Total "Urban" (Over 2500) Population (Thousands)*	*Per Cent Change in Decade*	*United States Population (Millions)*	*Per Cent Change in Decade*
1790	67.5	–	201.7	–	3,929.2	–
1800	153.2	127	322.4	60	5,308.5	35.0
1810	271.9	78	525.5	63	7,239.9	35.5
1820	359.9	32	693.3	32	9,638.4	33.1
1830	618.4	72	1,127.2	63	12,866.0	33.5
1840	972.2	57	1,845.1	64	17,069.5	32.7
1850	2,267.2	133	3,543.7	92	23,191.9	35.8
1860	5,011.7	122	6,216.5	75	31,443.3	35.6

Year of issue of directories was defined to include either the federal census year or the preceding year. Business directories were not included. The populations of a few small suburbs, particularly in the South, could not be determined since the areas were not separately returned in the census; but it is unlikely that the total population of areas thus omitted could affect the totals severely.

Sources: Spear, *Bibliography of American Directories Through 1860, passim.*; U.S. Census Office. Twelfth Census (1900), *Census Reports Volume I . . . Population Part I . . .,* 430-33; U.S. Census Office. Sixth Census (1840), *Sixth Census or Enumeration . . . 1840* (Washington: Blair & Rives, 1841), *passim.;* U.S. Census Office. Seventh Census (1850), *The Seventh Census of the United States: 1850 . . .* (Washington: Robert Armstrong, 1853), *passim.*; U.S. Census Office. Eighth Census (1860), *Population of the United States in 1860 . . .* (Washington: Government Printing Office, 1864), *passim.*; U.S. Bureau of the Census, *Historical Statistics of the United States Colonial Times to 1957* (Washington: Government Printing Office, 1961), 8, 14.

collector, accountant, and copyist. Adams bought out Stimpson as of 1847 and soon expanded his operations to include directories of Salem, Lowell, the suburb of Roxbury, and the "Environs of Boston," as well as a short-lived weekly business newspaper, the *Index of the City of Boston.* Adams's directories contained more features than did Stimpson's; chief among these was a classified business directory, a forerunner of today's "Yellow Pages." [5]

Adams's inclusion of a business directory in his city directories reflected one of at least three reasons for the appearance of city directories as a communications medium. Foremost, in an era of poor intra-urban communications, city directories aided the transaction of business; since there were few urban telegraph companies until after the Civil War, messengers took written communications from one office to another. Because of the constant movement of firms, the directory became outmoded in a year. The publisher counselled those thinking to make their old directories do that they should "consider that one or two blunders made in consequence of using a last year's Directory, may actually cost them more money than would buy several Directories." [6]

Secondly, one must assume the directories were intended by their projectors to be money-making ventures. But one should note that in many cities the directory appeared as a sideline of a printer, a stationer, or a newspaper. Complaints by directory-makers were legion:

> If but *half* of the merchants, doing a fair business, would buy a book, I could afford it at a $1 for a number of years to come, and receive, what I have a *right to expect*, a fair return for my labor. But when gentlemen merchants (if the word is not a solecism) will ask, and expect from me the labor and expense of making a book to guide the citizen and stranger to their stores and dwellings, and then run often ten rods to a more honorable neighbor, for "the Directory just a moment to find where Mr. Thompson lives," it affords but little encouragement.[7]

We cannot wonder at the extensive turnover in directory publishing.

Last, the directory served a "boomer" function, in that it advertised the benefits of its city to prospective residents and to those seeking an advantageous business location. But the directory served above all as a publication for businessmen, a fact we should not lose sight of, for it greatly affected content.

Before examining content, a word on compilation. The great advantage of the annual directory to the urban researcher is, of course, that it provides him with ten "snapshots" per decade of a large part of a city's population, rather than the two glimpses, admittedly much more comprehensive, he obtains from the federal census. Directory compilers got this information by an annual canvass of their cities, a task demanding patience and perseverance:

> *No Directory has been, or ever will be,* a correct estimate of the adult male population of any city. One warm election will do more in one day, in ascertaining this fact, than we can do in six months. All that the Compiler can do, is to visit every house, and carefully take down such information as he can obtain. When he has done this, he has done *all* that the public can reasonably expect of him. . . . there are a large number of people, who either from fear of doing militia duty, or from other causes, take effectual means of keeping their names from us.[8]

A directory publisher's later directories reveal some of his methods once he had passed the initial hurdle of his first directory. In the case of the Boston directories, it appears that Stimpson, and later Adams, sent out his canvassers carrying disbound copies of the previous year's directory, perhaps with each page pasted to a larger sheet of paper, allowing room for corrections and additions. It is clear that the typesetters who composed the Boston directories worked from corrected printed copy, for misalphabetizations carried on in some instances for several years. Had the canvassers not carried old directory pages, but blank paper instead, probably there would have been more misspellings of names but fewer misalphabetizations. Adams apparently was able, in his operation, to use his canvassers as clerks or copyists when the directory was not being prepared. In other cities, where the publication of a directory was a less well-established operation, one might see the following in a newspaper:

> Wants.
>
> AN AGENT of experience and good address will find profitable employment for a few weeks, by addressing "C.," 110 BALTIMORE STREET.[9]

Thus did the itinerant printer Daniel H. Craig, from New Hampshire, begin preparations for the Baltimore directory he published in 1842. By the next year he had sold out and moved on.[10]

The kinds of information directories provided about individuals usually included four basic items: name, occupation, home address, and work address. Occasionally, much more useful information would appear; for example, Cincinnati's 1840 directory gives the birthplace (by state or country) of many of its listees.[11] A close comparison of the Boston directories with other information sources indicates several conclusions one may draw from the presence or absence of various of these items of information. If only a home address appears, it is likely the individual was retired or had a menial occupation (usually laborer). In later years, though, one finds some merchants with this kind of listing. No work address usually indicates that the individual had no fixed work location, i.e., that his was an occasional occupation. This category would include most of Boston's laborers, but also a large proportion of such pliers of skilled occupations as masons and carpenters. Work address, but no home address, may mean the individual had recently moved. In Stimpson's Boston directories, it usually means that the person worked in Boston, but resided in a suburb. Adams began the practice of listing residence despite suburban location, choosing to ignore the implication that the city's better classes were seeking homes in the more salubrious suburbs (*cf.* Chapter VI). Sometimes, a person's home and work address appeared, but no occupation was listed. This practice started about the beginning of the 1850's in Boston, and seems to have been connected with the rise of a large group of salaried sales and clerical personnel, who for some reason did not want to be so identified. Their occupations must be inferred from the census or from a laborious matching of work address with the addresses of firms as given in the classified business directory. Sometimes after a few years the person would list his occupation in a later directory.

As one might anticipate of a communications medium intended

primarily for the use of businessmen, there was a distinct bias in the inclusivity of Boston's city directories. For instance, a detailed comparison of the 1830 and 1840 directories with the federal censuses of 1830 and 1840 for Ward 6 in Boston revealed that more than three-quarters of the white heads of household were listed in either directory, as against about one-seventh of the Negro household heads in 1830 and two-fifths in 1840 (see Table A-3).

Table A-3. Inclusivity of Boston City Directories of Heads of Household, by Race, Ward 6, 1830 and 1840[a]

	1830		*1840*	
Race of Household Head	*N*	*Per Cent Listed in 1830 Directory*	*N*	*Per Cent Listed in 1840 Directory*
White	639	81.2	1130	76.2
Negro	158	14.6	299	39.5
Total	797	68.0	1429	68.5

[a]Ward 6 was selected because it contained a majority of Boston's Negroes and because in the ward redistrictings of 1838 and 1850 (the latter inapplicable here) its boundaries were changed only slightly. The ward was bounded, approximately, by Cambridge, Beacon, and Court Streets and the Charles River.

Sources: City directories of Boston for 1830 and 1840; manuscript federal censuses of Boston, Ward 6, 1830 and 1840 (on microfilm from National Archives).

For Boston as a whole, and applying other criteria, a similar pattern emerges. There was a distinct economic bias in directory inclusion. Persons who were assessed for real and personal property worth less than a total of $1000 were less likely to appear in the directory than were individuals taxed for more than a total of $1000. Above the level of $1000, coverage by the directory was almost perfect (see Table A-4).

Coverage of the directories did not appear to suffer as Boston's population grew. If we divide the city into "core" and "peripheral" areas by assigning to the former the central business district ward and all adjacent wards, and by calling the periphery all remaining wards, we note in the ante-bellum era an accelerated growth of the peripheral wards, to the point at which they were accounting for over 97 per cent of Boston's net population growth (see

Table A-4. Inclusivity of Boston City Directories, 1830, 1840, 1850, and 1860, Compared with Level of City Tax Assessments (Sample Data)

	Property[a] Assessment Range (Current Dollars)				
	Under $200	*$200-$1000*	*$1001-$10,000*	*$10,001 and over*	*Total*
1830					
Number Assessed	128	60	50	19	257
Per Cent Listed in 1830 Directory	80.5	90.0	96.0	94.8	86.8
1840					
Number Assessed	120	73	74	21	288
Per Cent Listed in 1840 Directory	84.2	91.8	97.3	100.0	94.0
1850					
Number Assessed	140	36	39	31	246
Per Cent Listed in 1850 Directory	85.0	91.7	97.5	96.7	89.4
1860					
Number Assessed	142	26	50	34	252
Per Cent Listed in 1860 Directory	80.3	88.5	100.0	100.0	87.7

[a]"Property" is the total of real and personal property assessments, in current dollars.

Sources: Compiled from a random sample of 385 heads of households drawn from each of the federal manuscript censuses of Boston, 1830-60 (microfilms from National Archives), and traced through the Boston Assessors' Street (also known as "Taking" and "Valuation"), Transfer, and Tax volumes, Wards 1-12, 1830, 1840, 1850, and 1860 (Assessors' Vault, Boston City Hall), and the city directories for 1830, 1840, 1850, and 1860. The total number assessed does not add to 385 because in each year there were individuals resident in Boston who were not assessed and also others who were not subject to assessment (mostly widows), yet who were household heads and thus included in the sample.

Table A-5). In the face of such quickened growth at the edges of their city, Boston's directory compilers did well; in fact, their coverage of outlying areas was usually slightly better than that of the central areas (see Table A-6).

Table A-5. "Central" and "Peripheral" Population Changes in Boston, 1825-1837, 1837-1850, and 1850-1865[a]

Area	1. *1825* Population	2. *1837* Population	3. *Net Gain* *[(2)-(1)]*	4. *Net Gain as* *% of (1)*	5. *Net Gain as %* *of City Gain*
Center	25,101	32,210	7,109	28.3	31.5
Periphery	33,176	48,613	15,437	46.5	68.5
City	58,277	80,823	22,546	38.7	100.0
	1. *1837* Population	2. *1850* Population			
Center	46,221	60,647	14,426	31.2	24.9
Periphery	34,602	78,141	43,539	125.8	75.1
City	80,823	138,788	57,965	71.7	100.0
	1. *1850* Population	2. *1865* Population			
Center	74,279	75,688	1,409	1.9	2.6
Periphery	64,509	116,630	52,121	80.8	97.4
City	138,788	192,318	53,530	38.6	100.0

[a]Boston's wards were redistricted in 1838, 1850, and 1866; just before each redistricting, a census of the city was taken. The differing figures above for 1837 and 1850 reflect that redistricting. For definitions of "center" and "periphery," see Chapter II.

Sources: 1825, Lemuel Shattuck, *Report to the Committee of the City Council Appointed to Obtain the Census of Boston for the Year 1845. . .* (Boston: John H. Eastburn, 1846), Appendix 13; 1837, *Boston City Document No. 20* (1838), 5-10; 1850, *Boston City Document No. 42* (1850), 30; 1865, Massachusetts. Secretary of the Commonwealth, *Abstract of the Census of Massachusetts, 1865: With Remarks on the Same. . .* (Boston: Wright & Potter, 1867), 44.

Table A-6. "Central" and "Peripheral" City Directory Coverage, Boston, 1830, 1840, 1850, and 1860

	Area of Residence[a]		
	Center	*Periphery*	*City Total*
1830			
Number in sample[b]	145	240	385
Per Cent Listed in 1830 Directory	77.2	77.1	77.2
1840			
Number in Sample[b]	222	163	385
Per Cent Listed in 1840 Directory	80.2	84.0	81.8
1850			
Number in Sample[b]	160	225	385
Per Cent Listed in 1850 Directory	71.3	77.3	74.8
1860			
Number in Sample[b]	164	221	385
Per Cent Listed in 1860 Directory	72.0	72.9	72.4

[a]"Center" and "periphery" are defined in the accompanying text.
[b]The numbers in each sample coming from the center and periphery are proportional to the number of households in each area in the relevant federal census.

Sources: Sample of 385 heads of household selected from censuses of Boston for 1830, 1840, 1850, and 1860, as explained in source note for Table A-4; Boston city directories for 1830, 1840, 1850, and 1860.

Directories, properly used with an awareness of their racial, economic, areal, and other biases, can provide valuable data on internal urban conditions. But one must use them cautiously. For instance, Professor Sam B. Warner, Jr., in *The Private City: Philadelphia in Three Periods of Its Growth,* presents a comparison of occupational distributions for samples drawn from the 1860 census and from the 1860 city directory. He notes that the principal difference between the samples lies in the census sample's "inclusion of many more female occupations, domestics, housekeepers, seamstresses, tailoresses, and the male and female factory operatives." [12] To this we may add the categories of apprentices and other employed sons who remained members of the nuclear family.

The above should amply demonstrate that, from a methodological viewpoint, one should proceed from a census to a directory, and not *vice versa,* if he wishes to move from the more to the less complete. Of course, where the census has not survived, or is not yet available, city directories may serve as a makeshift.[13]

Among the uses of city directories, in addition to those already mentioned, are those of aids to indexing manuscript censuses, of adjuncts to traffic analysis, and of assistance in tracing the changing occupational trends of masses of individuals.

If the researcher expects to use a city's manuscript census returns quite extensively, he may find it advantageous to index the census returns by looking up, in the city directory for the census year, every *n*th household listed in the census. Arranging the results in the order of the census taker's visitation allows one to reconstruct the enumerator's peregrinations.[14] The greatest advantage in this method is that, given a person's name and address, and desiring to locate him in the manuscript returns, the researcher may consult his index and restrict his inquiry to only a few pages of the manuscript returns. Though the index compilation is onerous, it can pay large dividends in residential persistence studies.

By segregating all persons in the city directory who give both a home and a work address, one may derive some idea of the city's traffic patterns, at least for its higher economic strata, by plotting putative home-to-work paths on a map and summing the results for each street.

One may gain a notion of the occupational life styles of individuals in selected occupational categories by following those individuals through a number of consecutive city directories. Careful choice of a large number of persons in a particular occupation, and the tracing of these people over a period crucial to the development of their occupation, could provide much information on individuals' response to a changing work environment. For instance, how did shoemakers behave in the face of increased mechanization of their craft? Or, falling back momentarily to using directories as census indexers, what were the common characteristics of persons choosing a particular profession, for example, did the backgrounds of, say, telegraph operators differ from those of male workers generally, and if so, how? The directory would list many operators (depending on era and city size, of course), who could then be run to earth in the manuscript census. Again, one could use the directory to make a list of persons working in a given area but living elsewhere, then use the directory to find the persons in the census at their homes and extract data there. Other and analogous possibilities will occur to the reader.

Those willing to invest much effort in using city directories will derive a great return; but at the same time they should not hesitate to look these gift horses in the mouth.

Appendix B

A Method for Checking the Accuracy of Some Manuscript Census Data

Few studies which have exploited ante-bellum manuscript census data appear to have inquired into the accuracy or the completeness of those data.[1] None seems to have devised methods to make up for inadequacies, omissions, and errors in the census. This Appendix leaves aside the question of census completeness to concentrate upon and describe briefly one method of checking the accuracy of the manuscript census; it then applies the method to checking on age reporting in the 1850 and 1860 manuscript federal censuses of Boston.

The basic method used to supplement the shortcomings of manuscript federal census data was that of tracing. In this study, the 1540 sample members, it will be recalled, were drawn randomly from the manuscript federal censuses of Boston for 1830, 1840, 1850, and 1860. These persons were then traced through the Boston city directories for 1830–60, through the city property assessment records for 1830, 1840, 1850, and 1860, through the city death records, 1830–50, the state marriage records, 1841–60, the state birth records, 1841–60 (to detect parents from children's records), through the state death records, 1841–1910, through the 1850 and 1860 manuscript federal census returns for 128 Massachusetts towns and cities outside Boston (21 for 1850 only, 39 each for 1850 and 1860, and 29 for 1860 only), and, last, through the published *Vital Records* of 152 Massachusetts towns. Thus many individuals' data could be cross-checked with other, contemporaneous, information. Occupations, for instance, were not only listed in the 1850 and 1860 federal censuses, but also in all city directories, 1830–60, in the assessment records, and in the marriage, birth, and death records. In the 1850 and 1860 censuses, place of birth and age not only appeared, but were stated more explicitly, usually with town or city designated, in the marriage, birth, and death records, and in the *Vital Records* volumes. Addresses were listed not only in the city directories but also in assessment and birth records (see Table Int-1 for additional information). It was an unusual individual who managed entirely to escape all of the above listings.

The various sources thus provided "back-up" information on the individuals being studied. Since the individuals were a random sample of all heads of household in Boston as of 1830, 1840, 1850, and 1860, their characteristics, within limits, are those of all of Boston's heads of household in those years. Thus, errors and omissions of census and city directory data concerning sample members, when made good from supplementary information, provided means for checking the accuracy of city directories and the censuses. Both sources proved very accurate as to individuals' occupations. City directories were none too reliable as to addresses of foreign-born persons; this was due, of course, to their high residential mobility, discussed in Chapter IV. The censuses of 1850 and 1860 did manifest "age heaping," the tendency for reported ages to cluster around years ending in 0 and 5.

For many of the native-born sample members it was possible to learn their actual date of birth (day, month, year); foreign-born, mostly Irish, proved more difficult to check; subtraction of their ages, as reported in successive censuses, produced differences ranging from −5 to +20 years, leading to the conclusion that most of these people did not know how old they were. When native- and foreign-born persons' actual age at last birthday as of 1 June of the census year was computed and the absolute differ-

Table B-1. Absolute Difference Between Actual Age (Last Birthday Before 1 June of the Census Year) and Age Reported in Manuscript Federal Census Returns, for Members of 1850 and 1860 Sample Groups, 1850 and 1860

	1850 Census Sample Group					
Absolute Difference Between Actual and Reported Ages (Years)	*Total* *N*	*Per Cent*	*Native-Born* *N*	*Per Cent*	*Foreign-Born* *N*	*Per Cent*
0	49	26.9	40	28.2	9	22.5
1	71	39.0	59	41.5	12	30.0
2	19	10.4	17	12.0	2	5.0
3	18	9.9	12	8.5	6	15.0
4	5	2.7	4	2.8	1	2.5
5	4	2.2	1	0.7	3	7.5
6-10	12	6.6	6	4.2	6	15.0
11 and over	4	2.2	3	2.1	1	2.5
Sub-Total (Equals 100 Per Cent)	182		142		40	
Persons Whose Actual Age Could Not Be Determined	203		60		143	
Total	385		202		183	

	1860 Census Sample Group					
Absolute Difference Between Actual and Reported Ages (Years)	*Total* *N*	*Per Cent*	*Native-Born* *N*	*Per Cent*	*Foreign-Born* *N*	*Per Cent*
0	55	37.4	48	45.7	7	16.7
1	43	29.3	33	31.4	10	23.8
2	18	12.2	7	6.7	11	26.2
3	8	5.4	5	4.8	3	7.1
4	7	4.8	2	1.9	5	11.9
5	4	2.7	3	2.9	1	2.4
6-10	9	6.1	4	3.8	5	11.9
11 and over	3	2.0	3	2.9	–	–
Sub-Total (Equals 100 Per Cent)	147		105		42	
Persons Whose Actual Age Could Not Be Determined	238		66		172	
Total	385		171		214	

Source: Sample data.

ence between it and the reported age was found, the error distribution was as in Table B-1.

Roughly two-thirds to three-quarters of the native-born persons in the 1850 and 1860 censuses of Boston whose actual age could be determined either reported their correct age or were only one year off. For the foreign-born the proportion fell from about one-half in 1850 to about two-fifths in 1860. Since the enumerators probably asked "How old are you?" rather than "As of last June first, how old were you on your last preceding birthday?" this seems to be a very good showing. It is all the better when we note that in Boston the process of census-taking lasted from 30 July to 11 October in 1850, and from 1 June to 22 August in 1860. Persons whose birthdays fell in June, July, and August during 1860, and in those months plus September in 1850, would presumably have reported their "new" higher age to the enumerators. Assuming that, respectively, one-third and one-fourth of the individuals' birthdays fell in June–September and in June–August, this would have produced totals of about 25.0 per cent (in 1850) and 12.5 per cent (in 1860) of persons whose reported ages would have been one year high. Because the 1850 enumeration began two months late, one-sixth of the population would have celebrated birthdays in the interim. Since enumeration was continuous, individuals had an equal chance to be visited before or after their birthdays, so we must add another half of one-sixth, for a 25.0 per cent total. The 1860 census started on time, but ran for three months, or one-quarter year. Halving that produces the 12.5 per cent figure. In reality, 32 of 183 persons (17.5 per cent) in 1850, and 18 of 147 persons (12.3 per cent) in 1860, reported ages one year too high.

As a rule of thumb, then, this suggests that about two-thirds of Boston's adult population reported its age to the enumerators with an error of one year or less. About half of the adults seem to have reported their age at last birthday.

Appendix C

An Estimate of Census Under-Enumeration*

Most studies using census data accept them with minimal questioning of their accuracy. Researchers seldom have time, facilities, or (to be candid) the inclination to try to verify census data.[1] Furthermore, only the pre-1900 federal censuses are currently open to researchers and hence capable of being verified by comparing the manuscript returns with the printed results.

This Appendix essays an approximation of census under-enumeration in Boston for 1850 and 1860. Its methodology, of course, is generally applicable.

There were at least four components of Boston's non-enumerated population in 1850 and 1860:

A) persons residing in Boston during the census, not moving during the census, but nevertheless missed by the enumerators (presumably because "not at home;" but enumerators also seem to have missed quite a few corner houses, possibly in the belief they would be canvassed by someone else assigned to the other street);

B) persons residing in Boston as of 1 June (the census date), but moving away before enumerators reached them;

C) persons residing in Boston during the census, but moving

* A slightly different version of this Appendix appeared in *Historical Methods Newsletter* 3 (Dec. 1969), 5–8.

during the census from an unenumerated to an already enumerated area; and

D) persons residing in Boston as of 1 June, but dying before being enumerated.

To estimate these components, we must know some facts and make some assumptions. Enumeration of Boston lasted from 30 July to 11 October in 1850, and from 1 June to 22 August in 1860. Residential mobility of the population approximated 30 to 40 per cent annually. Of all annual moves, about 30 per cent were out-migratory. Since in-migration was usually about 10 per cent greater than out-migration, its share of annual moves was about 33 per cent, leaving circulation to account for 37 per cent of the moves. We assume that three-quarters of all moves occurred during the six warmer months, April–September. Since canvassing for the city directory and for city tax assessments both began in early May, activity was probably quite high during April. To promote conservative results, the following values will be used:

census duration: three months;
residential mobility: 30 per cent annually (symbol: m);
interdecadal persistence: 40 per cent (symbol: p).
Let

P_r = the reported population,
P_{ne} = the non-enumerated population, and
P_a = the "actual" or "real" population ($= P_r + P_{ne}$).

We estimate *A* (those missed by the enumerators) from the knowledge that in both the 1850 and 1860 censuses five sample members from earlier censuses (1.3 per cent) known to be present in Boston were missed by the enumerators. Since interdecadal persistence was 40 per cent, the 1.3 per cent figure should be multiplied by $\frac{1}{p}$ to correct for out-migration:

$$\frac{1}{p} \times 1.3 \text{ per cent} = 0.0325\, P_r.$$

Persons who left town during the census, component *B*, may be estimated by

$$P_a \times m \times 30 \text{ per cent} \times 0.75 \times 0.5 \times 0.5 = 0.563\, mP_a, \text{ or } 0.0169\, P_a,$$

after substituting for m. Those who left equaled $mP_a \times 30$ per cent (the out-migrating portion), but this must be further reduced by multiplying it by 0.75 (proportion of moves assumed to occur in April–September), by 0.5 (since the census lasted only three of those six months), and by 0.5 again, for the likelihood was equal that an enumerator would visit a home before or after its occupants' departure.

Component *C* depends upon the extent of population circulation, and may be estimated by

$$P_a \times m \times 37 \text{ per cent} \times 0.75 \times 0.5 \times 0.5, \text{ or } 0.0694\, mP_a;$$

this becomes 0.0208 P_a after substitution for m. The 37 per cent represents the proportion of moves attributable to circulation, while the other values are as in component *B*.

Although enumerators were supposed to count *D* (persons who had died between 1 June and the enumerator's visit), they did not do too well at this uncongenial task. Ordinarily, about 2.5 per cent of Boston's population (P_r) died each year. Assuming that one-quarter of the deaths occurred in the July–September period (the actual proportion in those three hot months during 1850–59 was 29.6 per cent[2]), we may approximate non-enumerated decedents by

$$0.025\, P_r \times 0.25 \times 0.5, \text{ or } 0.0031\, P_r,$$

which assumes equal likelihood of an enumerator's visit before or after an individual's death. It ignores as negligible the possibility of *D*'s members' also having been part of components *A* or *C*.

Accordingly,

$$P_{ne} = A + B + C + D, \text{ or}$$
$$P_{ne} = 0.0325\, P_r + 0.0169\, P_a + 0.0208\, P_a + 0.0031\, P_r.$$

Since

$P_a = P_r + P_{ne}$, we may substitute:
$P_a = P_r + 0.0356\ P_r + 0.0377\ P_a$; simplifying,
$0.9623\ P_a = 1.0356\ P_r$, or
$P_a = 1.076\ P_r$.

Our conservative estimate thus indicates an under-enumeration of 7.6 per cent. By varying the parameters slightly, we obtain different estimates:

mobility ratio (m) (per cent)	*proportion of moves (per cent)*			*estimated under-enumeration (per cent)*
	out-migratory	*in-migratory*	*circulatory*	
35	30	33	37	8.3
40	30	33	37	9.1
35	30	34.5	35.5	8.2
40	30	34.5	35.5	8.9

Another estimate, independently derived from city-directory alteration figures, gave these results:[3]

census	*estimated under-enumeration (per cent)*
1860	8.0
1885 (state)	9.7
1890	8.3

Because the two estimation procedures operated independently, it is pleasant to note their substantial agreement.

Others may care to examine under-enumeration problems in rural areas and in other cities.

Appendix D

Standard Error of Estimated Percentages

Estimated Percentage	*The chances are two out of three that this percentage differs from that of the total population by less than — per cent*
1 or 99	0.51
2 or 98	0.71
3 or 97	0.87
4 or 96	1.00
5 or 95	1.11
6 or 94	1.20
7 or 93	1.30
8 or 92	1.38
9 or 91	1.46
10 or 90	1.53
15 or 85	1.82
20 or 80	2.04
25 or 75	2.21
30 or 70	2.33
35 or 65	2.43
40 or 60	2.50
45 or 55	2.54
50	2.55

SOURCE: Calculated from the formula $\sqrt{\frac{p(1-p)}{N}}$, with N of 385.

Appendix E

Socioeconomic Classification of Occupations Encountered in This Study

Members of some occupations might have appeared in several classifications, according to their property valuation. In such cases, the occupation will be listed only once, with an indication of the other possible locations: for example, Barber/Hairdresser (also III and VII), listed under classification II, Semi-Skilled & Service. This would place most barbers and hairdressers in classification II except for those who possessed less than a total of $1000 in real and personal property, who would be assigned to classification III, Petty Proprietors, Managers, & Officials, or for those who owned property to a value of more than $1000, assigned to classification VII, Proprietors, Managers, & Officials.

I. *Unskilled & Menial Service*

Laborer
Housework
Porter
Laundress
Hostler/Stabler (also III, VII)

II. *Semi-Skilled & Service*

Steward
Waiter
Sexton (also III, VII)
Drain Digger
Seamstress/Dressmaker
Teamster (also III, VII)
Handcartman (also III, VII)
Mail Carrier
Policeman/Constable
Watchman
Fireman (City)
Butcher (also III, VII)
Cook
Servant
Sawyer
Barber/Hairdresser (also III, VII)
Dyer/Dye House (also III, VII)
Truckman (also III, VII)
Driver (also III, VII)
Expressman (also III, VII)
Hackman (also III, VII)
Paver
Lamplighter
Fisherman
Restauranteur/Restorator (also III, VII)

III. *Petty Proprietors, Managers, & Officials* (owning less than a total of $1000 in real and personal property)

Boarding House Proprietor (also VII)
Bath House Proprietor (also VII)
Contractor (also VII)
Marble Works Proprietor (also VII)

Merchant (Shoes) (also VII)
Merchant Tailor (also VII)
Merchant (Dry Goods) (also VII)
Hat Dealer (also VII)
Straw Goods & Bonnets (also VII)
Job Wagon Proprietor (also VII)
Merchant (Iron) (also VII)
Hotel Keeper or Manager (also VII)
Billiards Parlor Proprietor (also VII)
Merchant (Wood/Lumber) (also VII)
Shoe Dealer (also VII)
Merchant (Leather) (also VII)
Clothing Dealer/Dry or Fancy Goods Dealer (also VII)
Fur Dealer (also VII)
Pocket-Book Manufacturer (also VII)
Ship Chandlery Proprietor (also VII)
Horse Dealer
Railroad Conductor
Copper Dealer/Merchant (also VII)
Stove Dealer (also VII)
Merchant (Unspecified Product) (also VII)
Broker (also VII)
Inspector (Customs)/Weigher & Gauger
Carpet Dealer (also VII)
Hardware Dealer (also VII)
Coal Dealer (also VII)
Powder & Ammunition Dealer (also VII)
Periodicals Dealer (also VII)
Wine Bottler (also VII)
Merchant (Wines/Liquors) (also VII)
Grocery Proprietor (also VII)
Grocery/West Indies Goods Dealer/Merchant (also VII)
Produce Dealer (also VII)
Flour/Grain Dealer (also VII)
Chain Cable Factory Proprietor (also VII)
Peddler

Government Official (minor)
Chair Dealer (also VII)
Furniture Dealer (also VII)
Crockery Dealer (also VII)
Gas Fixtures Manufacturer (also VII)
Match Manufacturer (also VII)
Junk Dealer (also VII)
Publisher (also VII)
Organ Manufacturer (also VII)
Brewer (also VII)
Wines & Liquors Dealer (also VII)
Mustard Manufacturer (also VII)
Victualler (also VII)
Provisions Dealer (also VII)
Fish Dealer (also VII)
Oysterman (also VII)
Agricultural Implement & Seed Dealer (also VII)
Merchant (Drug) (also VII)
Saloon Proprietor (also VII)

IV. *Skilled*

Carpenter/Housewright (also III, VII)
Roofer (also III, VII)
Stair Builder (also III, VII)
Millwright (also III, VII)
Whitener & Colorer (also III, VII)
Stonecutter (also III, VII)
Shoemaker (also III, VII)
Currier (also III, VII)
Mason (also III, VII)
Lather/Plasterer (also III, VII)
Painter (All Kinds) (also III, VII)
Plumber (also III, VII)
Turner/Planer (also III, VII)
Slater (also III, VII)

Lastmaker (also III, VII)
Morocco Dresser (also III, VII)
Cloth Maker/Finisher (also III, VII)
Milliner (also III, VII)
Hatter (also III, VII)
Caulker & Graver (also III, VII)
Rigger (also III, VII)
Mastmaker (also III, VII)
Wheelwright/Carriagemaker/Coachmaker (also III, VII)
Railroad Brakeman
Coppersmith (also III, VII)
Silversmith (also III, VII)
Wireworker (also III, VII)
Whitesmith/Tinsmith (also III, VII)
Machinist (also III, VII)
Engineer/Boiler Tender
Stovemaker (also III, VII)
Stencil Cutter (also III, VII)
Cabinetmaker (also III, VII)
Chairpainter (also III, VII)
Crockery Packer
Glass Blower
Kerosene/Oil Refiner (also III, VII)
Brushmaker (also III, VII)
Printer (also III, VII)
Engraver (also III, VII)
Paper Stainer (also III, VII)
Baker (also III, VII)
Confectioner/Sugar-House Worker (also III, VII)
Cigarmaker (also III, VII)
Tailor/Tailoress (also III, VII)
Furrier (also III, VII)
Ship Carpenter (also III, VII)
Ropemaker (also III, VII)
Pump & Block Maker (also III, VII)
Sailmaker (also III, VII)

Ship Carver (also III, VII)
Harnessmaker (also III, VII)
Whipmaker (also III, VII)
Coachpainter (also III, VII)
Blacksmith (also III, VII)
Brassfinisher/Brass-Founder (also III, VII)
Moulder/Founder (also III, VII)
Philosophical Instrument Maker (also III, VII)
Cutler (also III, VII)
Boilermaker (also III, VII)
Inventor (also III, VII)
Upholsterer (also III, VII)
Carver (also III, VII)
Trunkmaker (also III, VII)
Gilder (also III, VII)
Paperhanger (also III, VII)
Lampmaker (also III, VII)
Tallow Chandler (also III, VII)
Jeweller/Watchmaker (also III, VII)
Truss Maker (also III, VII)
Stereotype Finisher (also III, VII)
Bookbinder (also III, VII)
Pianofortemaker (also III, VII)
Sausage Maker (also III, VII)
Chemical Worker

V. *Clerical & Sales*

Clerk (Store)/Tender/Salesman
Copyist
Collector
Agent (Shipping)/Freight
Auctioneer
Cashier/Bank Clerk
Messenger
Clerk (Office)

Accountant/Bookkeeper
Real Estate Agent
Agent (Unspecified & Miscellaneous)
Bookseller/Stationer (also III, VII)

VI. *Semi-Professional*

Entertainer/Musician
Nurse
Evangelist/Tract Society Representative
Comedian
Dentist
Architect
Artist

VII. *Proprietors, Managers, & Officials* (owning more than a total of $1000 in real and personal property)

Bridge Builder/Contractor
Wharfinger
Omnibus Proprietor
Insurance Company Official
Treasurer, Cotton Factory
Ship's Officer/Captain/Pilot
Railroad Superintendent
Banker
Government Official (Important)

VIII. *Professional*

Physician (Botanic Physician in VI)
Judge
Teacher/Music
Lawyer/Counsellor/Attorney
Clergyman
Editor
Druggist/Apothecary

IX. *Miscellaneous & Unknown*

Woman (No Occupation) as Head of Household (includes Widows)
Retired Male/"Gentleman"/Male Over 60, No Occupation
Unknown/No Occupation Listed

Notes

INTRODUCTION

1. "The Modern City as a Field of Historical Study," *in* Oscar Handlin and John Burchard, eds., *The Historian and the City* (Cambridge: M.I.T. Press, 1963), 26.
2. *Plain Folk of the Old South* (Baton Rouge: Louisiana State University Press, 1949; reprinted, Chicago: Quadrangle Paperbacks, 1965), 153.
3. "The Historian and the Computer: A Simple Introduction to Complex Computation," *Essex Institute Historical Collections* 104 (April 1968), 118.
4. Carroll D. Wright and William C. Hunt, *The History and Growth of the United States Census, Prepared for the Senate Committee on the Census* (Washington: Government Printing Office, 1900; reprinted, New York: Johnson Reprint Co., 1966), 12–52.
5. "Remarks upon the Schedules of 1850, etc.," *in* U.S. Census Office. Seventh Census (1850), *The Seventh Census of the United States: 1850. . . .* (Washington: Robert Armstrong, 1853), iv.
6. Herbert Arkin and Raymond R. Colton, comps., *Tables for Statisticians* (New York: Barnes & Noble, 1963), 145–46 (Table 20). Consult also Charles M. Dollar and Richard J. Jensen, *Historian's Guide to Statistics Quantitative Analysis and Historical Research* (New York: Holt, Rinehart & Winston, 1971).
7. Robert Gutman, "Birth and Death Registration in Massachusetts: II. The Inauguration of a Modern System, 1800–1849," *Milbank Memorial Fund Quarterly* 36 (Oct. 1958), 373–402; John B. Blake, "The Early History of Vital Statistics in Massachusetts," *Bulletin of the History of Medicine* 29 (Jan.–Feb. 1955), 46–68.

CHAPTER I

1. Boston *Daily Evening Transcript,* 24 July 1830, 1/1.
2. U. S. Congress. Senate. 21st Congress, 2nd Session (1830–31), Document No. 76 (serial volume 204), "Commerce and Navigation of the United States . . . ," 266–67.
3. Samuel G. Goodrich, *A System of Universal Geography* . . . (2 vols.; Boston: Carter, Hendee & Co., 1832), I, 55.
4. We ignore here the hamlet of Washington Village, annexed to Boston 21 May 1855, then with a population of 1319. *Boston City Document No. 69* (1856), 3.
5. Goodrich, *A System of Universal Geography,* I, 50.
6. *Boston City Document No. 18* (1847); *cf.* also editorial "South Boston" in Boston *Daily Evening Transcript,* 3 Dec. 1830, 2/1.
7. Boston *Daily Evening Transcript,* 30 Aug. 1830, 2/3.

CHAPTER II

1. *A Statistical View of the Population of Massachusetts, from 1765 to 1840* (Boston: Charles C. Little & James Brown, 1846), 3.
2. "Urbanization and Social Change; on Broadening the Scope and Relevance of Urban History," *in* Oscar Handlin and John Burchard, eds., *The Historian and the City* (Cambridge: M.I.T. Press, 1963), 236.
3. Boston. City Council, *The Railroad Jubilee* . . . (Boston: J. H. Eastburn, 1852), 268. As for the difference, "on Saturdays many leave for the country to pass the Sabbath." *American Railroad Journal* 24 (20 Sept. 1851), 597.
4. U. S. Census (1850), Schedule 1 (Population), Boston (microfilm from National Archives), *passim.*
5. U.S. Bureau of the Census, *Historical Statistics of the United States Colonial Times to 1957* (Washington: Government Printing Office, 1961), 14.
6. Percy W. Bidwell, "Population Growth in Southern New England, 1810–1860," *American Statistical Association Publications* 15 (Dec. 1917), 816.
7. *A Statistical View,* 78.
8. Massachusetts. Secretary of the Commonwealth, *Abstract of the Census of Massachusetts, 1865: With Remarks on the Same,* . . . (Boston: Wright & Potter, 1867), 274.
9. *Report to the Committee of the City Council Appointed to Obtain*

the Census of Boston for the Year 1845 . . . (Boston: John H. Eastburn, 1846), 26.
10. *Ibid.*, 27.
11. *Boston City Document No. 20* (1838), 2–3.
12. Calculated from figures in Shattuck, *Report to the Committee of the City Council*, 29–30.
13. Oscar Handlin, *Boston's Immigrants: A Study in Acculturation* (rev. ed.; Cambridge: Harvard University Press, 1959), 354, *n*.74.
14. Chickering, *A Statistical View*, 151–53.
15. *Ibid.*, 156.

CHAPTER III

1. *Report to the Committee of the City Council Appointed to Obtain the Census of Boston for the Year 1845* . . . (Boston: John H. Eastburn, 1846), 36.
2. Massachusetts. General Court. House. Session of 1856, Document No. 41, *Report of the Commissioners of Alien Passengers and Foreign Paupers. 1855.* (Boston: William White, 1856), 29; Locke's report, as Agent of the Alien Commissioners, was dated 15 January 1856.
3. Shattuck, *Report to the Committee of the City Council*, 36.
4. *Ibid.*, 37; Shattuck uses the terms "born of American parents" and "born of Foreign parents," neglecting those persons of "mixed" parentage. He does not say how the last were classified.
5. U. S. Census Office. Seventh Census (1850), *Statistical View of the United States, . . . A Compendium of the Seventh Census. . . .* (Washington: A. O. P. Nicholson, 1854), 399.
6. Massachusetts. Secretary of the Commonwealth, *Abstract of the Census of the Commonwealth of Massachusetts. . . . June, 1855.* . . . (Boston: William White, 1857), 126.
7. U. S. Census Office. Eighth Census (1860), *Population of the United States in 1860* . . . (Washington: Government Printing Office, 1864), 608.
8. *Report of the Joint Special Committee on the Census of Boston, May, 1855* . . . (Boston: Moore & Crosby, 1856), 9.
9. *Boston City Document No. 14* (1857), 10–11; *Boston City Document No. 9* (1858), 8; *Boston City Document No. 13* (1859), 5; *Boston City Document No. 85* (1860), 6–7.
10. The 1850 and 1860 figures are from Table III–11; that for 1855 is from Massachusetts. Secretary of the Commonwealth, *Abstract of the Census of . . . Massachusetts. . . . 1855*, 51, 232.

11. U. S. Census Office Seventh Census (1850), *The Seventh Census of the United States: 1850. . . .* (Washington: Robert Armstrong, 1853), xxxvi; U. S. Census Office. Eighth Census (1860), *Population of the United States in 1860,* 616–19.

CHAPTER IV

1. Cruft's report to the Executive Committee; Benevolent Fraternity of Churches, *Benevolent Fraternity of Churches; The Seventeenth Annual Report of the Executive Committee of the Benevolent Fraternity of Churches.* (Boston: John Wilson & Son, 1851), 5–6. Professor Tamara K. Hareven kindly called my attention to these reports.
2. Totals from the Boston city directories for 1831–1857; no figures are given for the years 1830, 1846, 1847, 1858, 1859, or 1860.
3. Appendix A evaluates the city directories' inclusion rates.
4. Lemuel Shattuck, *Report to the Committee of the City Council Appointed to Obtain the Census of Boston for the Year 1845 . . .* (Boston: John H. Eastburn, 1846), 162; *Boston City Documents Nos. 10* (1851), 11; 7 (1852), 14; *10* (1855), 12.
5. Everett S. Lee, "A Theory of Migration," *Demography* 3 (1966), 48.
6. George R. Taylor, "The Beginnings of Mass Transportation in Urban America," *Smithsonian Journal of History* 1 (Summer and Autumn 1966), 35–50, 31–54.
7. *Report of the Committee on the Expediency of Providing Better Tenements for the Poor* (Boston: Eastburn's Press, 1846), 13, 16.
8. *Boston City Document No. 42* (1850), 15.

CHAPTER V

1. *Annual Report of the Boston Society for the Prevention of Pauperism. Oct. 1, 1852.* (Boston: John Wilson & Son, 1852), 11–12.
2. "Commercial Cities and Towns of the United States. Number XXII. City of Boston," *Hunt's Merchants' Magazine* 23 (Nov. 1850), 496–97.
3. *Boston City Document No. 42* (1850), 49–50.
4. Boston. Assessing Department, Transfer Book for Ward 7, 1830, 21; Tax Book for Ward 10, 1840, 18; Tax Book for Ward 10, 1850, 45.
5. Arthur M. Johnson and Barry E. Supple, *Boston Capitalists and Western Railroads: A Study in the Nineteenth-Century Railroad Investment Process* (Cambridge: Harvard University Press, 1967), 46–47, 51, 83.
6. See the review of "success" literature in Stuart M. Blumin, "Mobility

in a Nineteenth-Century American City: Philadelphia, 1820–1860" (Dissertation, University of Pennsylvania, 1968), Chapter I.

7. (Boston: All the Booksellers, 1846).
8. By Thomas L. V. Wilson (Boston: The Author, 1848).
9. By Abner Forbes and James W. Greene (Boston: W. V. Spencer, 1851).
10. For an exception, see Chapter VI.
11. U. S. Bureau of the Census, *Historical Statistics of the United States Colonial Times to 1957* (Washington: Government Printing Office, 1961), 127.
12. Boston. Board of Trade, *Eighth Annual Report* . . . (Boston: Alfred Mudge & Son, 1862), 109.
13. *Boston City Document No.* 9 (1842), 3–4.
14. Professor Stephan Thernstrom devised the classification for his *Migration and Social Mobility in Boston, 1880–1968: A Study in the New Urban History* (Cambridge: Harvard University Press, 1971). He generously permitted its use in this study.
15. Boston. Assessing Department, "Directions For Assessing Taxes," undated, pasted in front of Street Book for Ward 1, 1860, and many other Street Books. However, stockholders in banks and insurance companies were assessed, according to "Finances of Boston —Property and Taxes," *Hunt's Merchants' Magazine* 29 (Dec. 1853), 730–31.
16. *Boston City Document No. 60* (1851), 54, 57, 58.

CHAPTER VI

1. "Commercial Cities and Towns of the United States. Number XXII. City of Boston," *Hunt's Merchants' Magazine* 23 (Nov. 1850), 485.
2. *Twentieth Annual Report of the Boston Society for the Prevention of Pauperism. October, 1855* (Boston: John Wilson & Son, 1855), 12*n*.
3. Stuart M. Blumin, "Mobility in a Nineteenth-Century American City: Philadelphia, 1820–1860" (Dissertation, University of Pennsylvania, 1968), 107; Blake McKelvey, *Rochester: The Flower City 1855–1890* (Cambridge: Harvard University Press, 1949), 3*n*.
4. Peter R. Knights, "Population Turnover, Persistence, and Residential Mobility in Boston, 1830–60," *in* Stephan Thernstrom and Richard Sennett, eds., *Nineteenth-Century Cities: Essays in the New Urban History* (New Haven: Yale University Press, 1969), 271–74.
5. Stephan Thernstrom, "Urbanization, Migration, and Social Mobility in Late Nineteenth-Century America," *in* Barton J. Bernstein, ed.,

Towards A New Past: Dissenting Essays in American History (New York: Pantheon Books, 1968), 167.

6. *Boston City Document No. 42* (1850), 13–14; this suggests that "middle-class flight to the suburbs" is not new.
7. U. S. Census Office. Seventh Census (1850), *The Seventh Census of the United States: 1850 . . .* (Washington: Robert Armstrong, 1853), xxxvi; U.S. Census Office. Eighth Census (1860), *Population of the United States in 1860 . . .* (Washington: Government Printing Office, 1864), xxxiii–xxxv, 616–19.
8. See, for example, Boston *Daily Evening Transcript,* 27 June 1846, 4/1.
9. *Boston City Document No. 42* (1850), 39.
10. *Boston City Document No. 11* (1852), 3 (sentence order changed).
11. Charles J. Kennedy, "Commuter Services in the Boston Area, 1835–1860," *Business History Review* 36 (Summer 1962), 168–69.
12. Quoted from §15 of "An Act Providing for the Taking of the Seventh and Subsequent Censuses of the United States . . . ," cited in U.S. Census Office. Seventh Census (1850), *The Seventh Census of the United States: 1850,* xx.
13. *Cf.* Blumin, *op. cit.* (in Note 3), Chapter III.

CHAPTER VII

1. "Urbanization and Social Change; on Broadening the Scope and Relevance of Urban History" *in* Oscar Handlin and John Burchard, eds., *The Historian and the City* (Cambridge: The M.I.T. Press, 1963), 236.
2. See Great Britain. Interdepartmental Committee on Social and Economic Research, *Guides to Official Sources No. 2 Census Reports of Great Britain 1801–1931* (London: His Majesty's Stationary Office, 1951); also W. A. Armstrong, "The Interpretation of the Census Enumerators' Books for Victorian Towns," *in* Harold J. Dyos, ed., *The Study of Urban History* (London: Edward Arnold Ltd., 1968), 82, *n.*18, suggests that British manuscript censuses are less informative for social mobility studies than are American manuscript censuses. (I am indebted to Professor Lampard for these references.)

APPENDIX A

1. Research Publications, Inc., P.O. Box 3903, Amity Station, New Haven, Connecticut 06525.
2. Worcester, Mass.: American Antiquarian Society, 1961.
3. This discounts the statement in Stuart M. Blumin, "Mobility in a Nineteenth-Century American City: Philadelphia, 1820–1860," (Dis-

sertation, University of Pennsylvania, 1968), 87, that the Philadelphia city directories of 1830, 1840, and 1850 "contain only some 55 per cent of the adult male population." This appears to be an estimate, since it stands without supporting data. I wish to thank Professor Blumin for sending me a copy of his dissertation.

4. Among those studies which have used nineteenth-century city directories extensively the following may be noted: George H. Evans, Jr., "A Sketch of American Business Organization, 1832–1900," *Journal of Political Economy* 60 (Dec. 1952), 475–86; George H. Evans, Jr., and Walter C. Kanwisher, Jr., "Business Organization in Baltimore, 1859," *Journal of Political Economy* 62 (Feb. 1954), 63–67; Ruth G. Hutchinson, Arthur R. Hutchinson, and Mabel Newcomer, "A Study in Business Mortality: Length of Life of Business Enterprises in Poughkeepsie, New York, 1843–1936," *American Economic Review* 28 (Sept. 1938), 497–514.
5. Spear, *Bibliography,* 49–57. Information on Stimpson comes from federal manuscript census returns for Dorchester, Mass. (1850, household number 772; 1860, household number 2428), and from the state death records (vol. 221, p. 251). Stimpson was born in 1793 and died in 1869. Adams was born in Boston in 1807 and died there in 1865. (His returns are: 1850, Boston, Ward 11, household number 117; 1860, Newton, Mass., household number 2270.) Details of Adams' operations may be found in his directories for 1847, pp. 2, 8, and 1851, p. 272, while an obituary is in the 1866 directory, pp. 3–4.
6. *The Boston Directory . . . for . . . 1861* (Boston: Adams, Sampson, & Co., 1861), 2.
7. *Hoffman's Albany Directory, and City Register, for the Years 1845–6* (Albany: L. G. Hoffman, 1845), 19.
8. *Ibid.,* 18–19. For other comments, see "Commercial Directories," *Hunt's Merchants' Magazine and Commercial Review* 27 (Aug. 1852), 262–63, and "The New York City Directory," *ibid.,* 28 (June 1853), 772.
9. Baltimore *Sun,* 27 Nov. 1841, 3/3 (top).
10. The career of Daniel H. Craig (1811–95) certainly deserves biographical treatment. His importance to the development of early American communication media was very great, and is only adumbrated in the *Dictionary of American Biography* (20 vols.; New York: Charles Scribner's Sons, 1928–37), IV, 495–96.
11. Spear, *Bibliography,* 101. Professor Walter Glazer, University of Pittsburgh, kindly called my attention to this unusual directory feature.
12. Philadelphia: University of Pennsylvania Press, 1968, pp. 227–28.

Professor Warner was good enough to send me copies of these tables four months before his book's publication.

13. For an example, see Paul B. Worthman, "Working Class Mobility in Birmingham, Alabama, 1880–1914," *in* Tamara K. Hareven, ed., *Anonymous Americans: Explorations in Nineteenth-Century Social History* (Englewood Cliffs, N.J.: Prentice-Hall, 1971), 172–213.
14. *Cf.* Michael P. Conzen, "Spatial Data from Nineteenth Century Manuscript Censuses: A Technique for Rural Settlement and Land Use Analysis," *Professional Geographer* 21 (Sept. 1969), 337–43.

APPENDIX B

1. An outstanding exception to this statement has recently appeared: Margaret Walsh, "The Census as an Accurate Source of Information: The Value of Mid-Nineteenth Century Returns," *Historical Methods Newsletter* 3 (Sept. 1970), 3–13.

APPENDIX C

1. See, for example, Sam B. Warner, Jr., *Streetcar Suburbs: The Process of Growth in Boston, 1870–1900* (Cambridge: Harvard University Press, 1962), 171–78; Edgar Z. Palmer, "The Correctness of the 1890 Census of Population for Nebraska Cities," *Nebraska History* 32 (Dec. 1951), 259–67; and Thomas H. Hollingsworth, *Historical Demography* (Ithaca: Cornell University Press, 1969, 107–8.
2. From 1850 to 1859, inclusive, 39,882 persons were reported as having died in Boston. Of these, 11,800 (29.59 per cent) died in the months of July, August, and September. See *Boston City Document No. 10* (1851), 19; *No. 7* (1852), 13; *No. 10* (1853), 12; *No. 12* (1854), 16; *No. 10* (1855), 13, 14; *No. 10* (1856), 13, 18; *No. 14* (1857), 22, 23; *No. 9* (1858), 18, 19; *No. 13* (1859), 14, 17; and *No. 85* (1860), 20, 23. (There was no report published covering the year 1860.) Boston's 1850 population was 138,788; in 1860, 177,840. The arithmetic mean was 158,314, and 3,988 (average annual deaths) is 2.52 per cent of that.
3. Data calculated for, but not used in, Stephan Thernstrom and Peter R. Knights, "Men in Motion: Some Data and Speculations About Urban Population Mobility in Nineteenth-Century America," *Journal of Interdisciplinary History* 1 (Autumn 1970), 7–35, and *in* Tamara K. Hareven, ed., *Anonymous Americans: Explorations in Nineteenth-Century Social History* (Englewood Cliffs, N.J.: Prentice-Hall, 1971), 17–47.

Bibliography

This list names those materials most useful in the writing of this study. Many citations of peripheral or negligible importance were suppressed in the interest of concision. The series of *Vital Records* volumes which exists for over 160 communities (of which 152 were searched) proved invaluable.

Unpublished Materials

Blumin, Stuart M. "Mobility in a Nineteenth-Century American City: Philadelphia, 1820–1860." Dissertation, University of Pennsylvania, 1968.

Boston. Mount Hope Cemetery. "Index of Interments." Vol. I, Mount Hope Cemetery, 1852–82.

———. "Private Lots and Graves: Record of Interments." Vol. I (18 May 1852–12 Oct. 1863; Nos. 1–1890); Vol. II (15 Oct. 1863–31 Dec. 1881; Nos. 1891–10, 277).

Boston. Registrar's Office. "Births Registered in the City of Boston from 1800 to 1848 Inclusive."

———. "City of Boston. Consolidated Index of Births 1849 to 1869 Inclusive." 7 vols.: A–C, D–F, G–K, L–M, N–R, S, T–Z.

———. "Boston Alphabetical Death Records 1801 to 1848 Inclusive." 5 vols.: A–D, E–H, I–M, N–S, T–Z.

———. "City of Boston. Index of Deaths 1849 to 1869 Inclusive." 4 vols.: A–D, E–K, L–P, Q–Z.

———. "City of Boston. Index of Deaths 1870 to 1881 Inclusive." 4 vols.: A–D, E–K, L–P, Q–Z.

———. "City of Boston Consolidated Index of Marriages 1800 to 1849 Inclusive." 2 vols.: A–J, K–Z.
———. "City of Boston, Consolidated Index of Marriages 1849 to 1859 Inclusive." 6 vols.: A–C, D–G, H–L, M–O, P–S, T–Z.
Madden, Carl H. "The Growth of the Cities in the United States: An Aspect of the Development of an Economic System." Dissertation, University of Virginia, 1954.
Massachusetts. Secretary of the Commonwealth. Division of Vital Statistics. Records of Births, Deaths, and Marriages, 1841–1903 (part). 541 vols.
———. Record of Deaths, 1903 (part)–1910. 805 vols.
———. "Index to Births in Massachusets 1841–1850." 4 vols.: Abbe–Dillon, Dilloway–Kenrick, Kent–Roarke, Robarts–Zeller.
———. "Index to Births in Massachusetts 1851–1855." 4 vols.: Aael–Dockett, Dockham–Kelsh, Kelso–Putney, Pye–Zutt.
———. "Index to Births in Massachusetts 1856–1860." 5 vols.: Aarens–Cyren, Dablen–Hincke, Hinckley–Mulry, Mulstee–Shores, Shorey–Zwinger.
———. "Index to Deaths in Massachusetts 1841–1850." 3 vols.: Aaron–Fuller, Gage–Parker, Parkhurst–Zumgrunde.
———. "Index to Deaths in Massachusetts 1851–1855." 3 vols.: Aames–Guilford, Gullivan–Richards, Richardson–Zumgrunde.
———. "Index to Deaths in Massachusetts 1856–1860." 3 vols.: Aarnson–Gigger, Gilbert–Pelan, Peland–Zuyll.
———. "Index to Deaths in Massachusetts 1861–1865." 4 vols.: Aaron–Emerton, Emery–Larrabee, Lasher–Richard, Richards–Zuza.
———. "Index to Deaths in Massachusetts 1866–1870." 3 vols.: Aaron–Freeborn, Freedburg–Myslinski, Nabba–Zweckler.
———. "Index to Deaths in Massachusetts 1871–1875." 4 vols.: Aantorn–Dorsy, Dorthey–Kyne, Labadoni–Quyney, Rabadeau–Zwinger.
———. "Index to Deaths in Massachusetts 1876–1880." 4 vols.: Aalders–Dill, Dill–Keiser, Keistead–Plance, Pland–Zwisler.
———. "Index to Deaths in Massachusetts 1881–1885." 4 vols.: Aaiken–Dimmick, Dimmock–Kinnane, Kinnard–Ponton, Pool–Zwinger.
———. "Index to Deaths in Massachusetts 1886–1890." 5 vols.: Aames–Cronan, Cronan–Hanna, Hannaberry–McDermott, McDermott–Rooker, Rooks–Zwinger.
———. "Index to Deaths in Massachusetts 1891–1895." 6 vols.: Aakkunami–Collar, Collard–Frepanier, Frepanier–Kibbee, Kibble–Mulverhill, Mulvey–Searing, Searl–Zytkiewicz.

———. "Index to Deaths in Massachusetts 1896–1900." 6 vols.: Aaron–Colburne, Colby–Fusco, Fusonia–Klose, Kloseman–Mountford, Mountfort–Shankland, Shankland–Zytkiewicz.

———. "Index to Deaths in Massachusetts 1901–1905." 6 vols.: Aaron–Clucher, Cluck–Gadren, Gadsby–Kirchler, Kirchner–Mundy, Munford–Shalvey, Sham–Zywa.

———. "Index to Deaths in Massachusetts 1906–1910." 7 vols.: Aaltonen–Cassabona, Cassadou–Estey, Estis–Homai, Homan–Mangano, Mangelwicz–Paessoent, Paetz–Smiledge, Smiley–Zyzkowska.

———. "Index to Marriages in Massachusetts 1841–1850." 3 vols.: Aaron–Hadley, Hadlock–Rutter, Ryan–Zuill.

———. "Index to Marriages in Massachusetts 1851–1855." 3 vols.: Aarnold–Finney, Finnigan–McMahone, McMahoney–Zyroth.

———. "Index to Marriages in Massachusetts 1856–1860." 3 vols.: Aams–Forcey, Ford–Mulliken, Mullin–Zwicker.

Rosen, Elliot A. "The Growth of the American City, 1830 to 1860: Economic Foundations of Urban Growth in the Pre-Civil War Period." Dissertation, New York University, 1953.

U. S. Census (1830). Schedules of Population, Boston, Massachusetts (Microfilm from National Archives).

U. S. Census (1840). Schedules of Population, Boston and Chelsea, Massachusetts (Microfilm from National Archives).

U. S. Census (1850). Schedule 1 (Population), Boston, Arlington, Beverly, Billerica, Bolton, Boylston, Brighton, Brookfield, Brookline, Burlington, Cambridge, Charlestown, Chelsea, Chicopee, Dedham, Dennis, Dorchester, Duxbury, Fitchburg, Grafton, Haverhill, Heath, Hingham, Holyoke, Hubbardston, Hull, Lawrence, Leominster, Lexington, Lowell, Lunenburg, Lynn, Medford, Melrose, Methuen, Milford, New Bedford, Newburyport, Newton, North Chelsea, Norwell, Oakham, Phillipston, Quincy, Reading, Roxbury, Saugus, Scituate, Shirley, Somerville, Springfield, Sterling, Sudbury, Templeton, Waltham, Watertown, Westboro', Wilmington, Winchester, Woburn, Worcester, Massachusetts (Microfilm from National Archives).

———. Schedule 5 (Manufactures), Boston, Massachusetts (Microfilm from Massachusetts Archives).

U. S. Census (1860). Schedule 1 (Population), Boston, Andover, Arlington, Ashland, Belmont, Beverly, Billerica, Boylston, Braintree, Brighton, Brockton, Brookline, Cambridge, Canton, Charlestown, Chelsea, Chicopee, Cohasset, Concord, Dedham, Dorchester, Dover, Duxbury, Fitchburg, Framingham, Gloucester, Groton, Hingham, Ipswich, Lawrence, Lexington, Lincoln, Lowell, Lunenburg, Lynn, Malden, Medford, Melrose, Methuen, Milton, Nahant, Natick, Needham, Newburyport, Newton, North Chelsea, Norwell, Phillipston, Plymouth, Quincy, Randolph, Reading, Roxbury, Salem, Sandwich, Saugus, Scituate, Sherborn, Somerville, Stoneham, Sudbury, Waltham, Watertown, Wayland, Weston, West Roxbury, Weymouth, Winchester, Woburn, Massachusetts (Microfilm from National Archives).

Ward, David. "Nineteenth Century Boston: A Study in the Role of Antecedent and Adjacent Conditions in the Spatial Aspects of Urban Growth." Dissertation, University of Wisconsin, 1963.

Woodlawn Cemetery (Everett, Mass.). "Record of Interments in Woodlawn Cemetery." Vol. I (30 June 1851–3 July 1867; Nos. 1–5000). Vol. II (5 July 1867–14 April 1876; Nos. 5001–10,000). Vol. III (15 April 1876–31 Aug. 1884; Nos. 10,001–15,000). Vol. IV (31 Aug. 1884–1 May 1891; Nos. 15,001–20,000). Vol. VIII (21 Sept. 1907–8 Nov. 1912; Nos. 35,001–40,000). Vol. IX (9 Nov. 1912–22 Oct. 1917; Nos. 40,001–45,000).

Published Materials

GOVERNMENT PUBLICATIONS

Boston. *Boston City Documents.* Boston: various publishers, 1834–1861. Especially useful documents are cited individually below.

Boston. Censors Appointed by the Board of Mayor and Aldermen to Obtain the State Census of Boston, May 1, 1850. *Report [an]d Tabular Statement of the Censors Appointed by the Board of Mayor and Aldermen, to Obtain the State Census of Boston, May 1, 1850. Also, a Letter from Jesse Chickering, M. D. in Reference to the Same. Boston City Document No. 42;* Boston: John H. Eastburn, 1850.

Boston. City Council. *The Charter and Ordinances of the City of Boston, Together with the Acts of the Legislature Relating to the City, and an Appendix. Published by Order of the City Council.* Boston: Moore & Crosby, 1856.

———. *The Charter and Ordinances Of the City of Boston, Together with the Acts of the Legislature Relating to the City: Collated and Revised Pursuant to an Order of the City Council, by Peleg W. Chandler.* Boston: John H. Eastburn, 1850.

———. *The Charter and Ordinances Of the City of Boston, Together with the Acts of the Legislature Relating to the City. Collated and Revised, Pursuant to an Order of the City Council, by Thomas Wetmore and Edward G. Prescott Commissioners.* Boston: J. H. Eastburn, 1834.

———. *The Railroad Jubilee. An Account of the Celebration Commemorative of the Opening of Railroad Communication Between Boston and Canada, September 17th, 18th, and 19th, 1851.* Boston: J. H. Eastburn, 1852.

Boston. Clerk of Committees. *Index to the City Documents 1834 to 1909 . . .* Boston: City Printing Department, 1910.

Boston. Committee Appointed by the City Council (1850). *Report of the Committee Appointed by the City Council; and also a Comparative View of the Population of Boston in 1850, with the Births, Marriages, and Deaths, in 1849 and 1850, by Jesse Chickering, M.D. Boston City Document No. 60;* Boston: J. H. Eastburn, 1851.

Boston. Committee of Internal Health. *Report of the Committee of Internal Health on the Asiatic Cholera, Together with a Report of the City Physician on the Cholera Hospital. Boston City Document No. 66;* Boston: J. H. Eastburn, 1849.

Boston. Joint Special Committee on the Census of Boston, May, 1855. *Report of the Joint Special Committee on the Census of Boston, May, 1855, Including the Report of the Censors, With Analytical and Sanitary Observations. By Josiah Curtis, M. D.* Boston: Moore & Crosby, 1856.

Dubester, Henry J. (comp.) *Catalog of United States Census Publications 1790–1945.* Washington: Bureau of the Census, 1950.

Gettemy, Charles F. *An Historical Survey of Census Taking in Massachusetts Including a Sketch of the Various Methods Adopted from Time to Time Since 1780 for Determining and Apportioning the Membership of the House of Representatives and the Senate and Council.* Boston: Wright & Potter Printing Co., 1919.

Great Britain. Interdepartmental Committee on Social and Economic Research. *Guides to Official Sources No. 2 Census Reports of Great Britain 1801–1931.* London: His Majesty's Stationery Office, 1951.

Massachusetts. Bureau of Statistics of Labor. *History of Wages and Prices in Massachusetts: 1752–1883. Including Comparative Wages and Prices in Massachusetts and Great Britain: 1860–1883. [Being Parts III. and IV. of the Sixteenth Annual Report of the Massachusetts Bureau of Statistics of Labor.] By Carroll D. Wright, Chief of the Bureau of Statistics of Labor.* Boston: Wright & Potter Printing Co., 1885.

Massachusetts. General Court. House (Session of 1856). Document No. 41. *Report of the Commissioners of Alien Passengers and Foreign Paupers. 1855.* Boston: William White, 1856.

Massachusetts. Sanitary Commissioners. *Report of a General Plan for the Promotion of Public and Personal Health, Devised, Prepared and Recommended by the Commissioners Appointed Under a Resolve of the Legislature of Massachusetts, Relating to a Sanitary Survey of the State. Presented April 25, 1850.* Boston: Dutton & Wentworth, 1850.

Massachusetts. Secretary of the Commonwealth. *Abstract of the Census of Massachusetts, 1860, from the Eighth U. S. Census, with Remarks on the Same. Prepared under the Direction of Oliver Warner, Secretary of the Commonwealth, by George Wingate Chase.* Boston: Wright & Potter, 1863.

———. *Abstract of the Census of Massachusetts, 1865: With Remarks on the Same, and Supplementary Tables. Prepared Under the Direction of Oliver Warner, Secretary of the Commonwealth.* Boston: Wright & Potter, 1867.

———. *Abstract of the Census of the Commonwealth of Massachusetts, Taken with Reference to Facts Existing on the First Day of June, 1855. With Remarks on the Same. Prepared under the direction of Francis DeWitt, Secretary of the Commonwealth.* Boston: William White, 1857.

———. . . . *Annual Report of the Secretary of the Commonwealth to the Legislature: Under the Act of March, 1842, Relating to the Registry and Returns of Births, Marriages and Deaths in Massachusetts. . . .* (Titles vary slightly.) Boston: Dutton & Wentworth, 1843–51; White & Potter, 1852; William White, 1853–62.

———. *Historical Data Relating to Counties, Cities and Towns in Massachusetts.* Boston: [Commonwealth of Massachusetts], 1966.

———. *Statistical Information Relating to Certain Branches of Industry in Massachusetts, for the Year Ending June 1, 1855. Prepared from Official Returns, by Francis DeWitt, Secretary of the Commonwealth.* Boston: William White, 1856.

———. *Statistical Information Relating to Certain Branches of Industry in Massachusetts, for the Year Ending May 1, 1865. Prepared from Official Returns, by Oliver Warner, Secretary of the Commonwealth.* Boston: Wright & Potter, 1866.

———. *Statistical Tables: Exhibiting the Condition and Products of Industry in Massachusetts, for the Year Ending April 1, 1837* Boston: Dutton & Wentworth, 1838.

———. *Statistics of the Condition and Products of Certain Branches of Industry in Massachusetts, for the Year Ending April 1, 1845. Prepared from the Returns of the Assessors by John G. Palfrey, Secretary of the Commonwealth.* Boston: Dutton & Wentworth, 1846.

Middlesex County, Massachusetts. Probate Court. *Index to the Probate Records of the County of Middlesex Massachusetts First Series From 1648 to 1871.* Cambridge: No Publisher, 1914.

Rhode Island. Superintendent of the Census. *Rhode Island State Census, 1885. (Advance Sheets.)* Providence: Census Office, 1886.

Shattuck, Lemuel. *Report to the Committee of the City Council Appointed to Obtain the Census of Boston for the Year 1845, Embracing Collateral Facts and Statistical Researches, Illustrating the History and Condition of the Population, and Their Means of Progress and Prosperity.* Boston: John H. Eastburn, 1846.

Suffolk County, Massachusetts. Probate Court. *Index to the Probate Records of the County of Suffolk, Massachusetts. From the Year 1636 to and Including the Year 1893.* 3 vols.; Boston: Rockwell & Churchill, 1895.

U. S. Bureau of the Census. *American Census Taking from the First Census of the United States.* Washington: Government Printing Office, n. d. [1903?].

———. *Historical Statistics of the United States Colonial Times to 1957.* Washington: Government Printing Office, 1961.

———. *Historical Statistics of the United States Colonial Times to 1957 Continuation to 1962 and Revisions A Statistical Abstract Supplement* Washington: Government Printing Office, 1965.

———. Twelfth Census (1900). *Census Reports Volume I Twelfth Census of the United States, Taken in the Year 1900 . . . Population Part I.* Washington: U. S. Census Office, 1901.

U. S. Census Office. First Census (1790). *Return of the Whole Number of Persons Within the Several Districts of the United States, According to "An Act Providing for the Enumeration of the Inhabitants of the United States," Passed March the First, One Thousand Seven Hundred and Ninety-One.* Philadelphia: Childs & Swaine, 1791.

U. S. Census Office. Second Census (1800). *Return of the Whole Number of Persons Within the Several Districts of the United States, According to "An act providing for the second Census or Enumeration of the Inhabitants of the United States." Passed*

February the twenty eighth, one thousand eight hundred. Washington: William Duane & Son, 1801.

U. S. Census Office. Third Census (1810). *Aggregate amount of each description of Persons within the United States of America, and the Territories thereof, agreeably to actual enumeration made according to law, in the year 1810.* [Washington: no publisher, 1811].

U. S. Census Office. Fourth Census (1820). *Census for 1820. Published by authority of an Act of Congress, under the direction of the Secretary of State.* Washington: Gales & Seaton, 1821.

U. S. Census Office. Fifth Census (1830). *Fifth Census; or, Enumeration of the Inhabitants of the United States, as Corrected at the Department of State, 1830. Published by authority of an Act of Congress, under the direction of the Secretary of State.* Washington: Duff Green, 1832.

U. S. Census Office. Sixth Census (1840). *Sixth Census or Enumeration of the Inhabitants of the United States, as Corrected at the Department of State, in 1840. Published, by Authority of an Act of Congress, Under the Direction of the Secretary of State.* Washington: Blair & Rives, 1841.

U. S. Census Office. Seventh Census (1850). *The Seventh Census of the United States: 1850. Embracing a Statistical View of Each of the States and Territories, Arranged by Counties, Towns, Etc., under the Following Divisions: . . . With an Introduction, Embracing the Aggregate Tables for the United States Compared with Every Previous Census Since 1790—Schedules and Laws of Congress Relating to the Census in the Same Period—Ratio Tables of Increase and Decrease of Cities and States, Etc., by Sex and Ages, and Color—Table of Population of Every County, Town, Township, Etc., in the United States, Alphabetically Arranged—Together with Some Explanatory Remarks, and an Appendix, Embracing Notes upon the Tables of Each of the States, Etc. J. D. B. DeBow, Superintendent of the United States Census.* Washington: Robert Armstrong, 1853.

———. *The Seventh Census. Report of the Superintendent of the Census for December 1, 1852; to Which is Appended the Report for December 1, 1851. Printed by Order of the House of Representatives of the United States.* Washington: Robert Armstrong, 1853.

———. *Statistical View of the United States, Embracing its Territory, Population—White, Free Colored, and Slave—Moral and Social Condition, Industry, Property, and Revenue; The Detailed Sta-*

tistics of Cities, Towns and Counties; Being a Compendium of the Seventh Census, to Which Are Added the Results of Every Previous Census, Beginning with 1790, in Comparative Tables, with Explanatory and Illustrative Notes, Based upon the Schedules and Other Official Sources of Information. By J. D. B. DeBow, Superintendent of the United States Census. Washington: A. O. P. Nicholson, 1854.

U. S. Census Office. Eighth Census (1860). *Manufactures of the United States in 1860; Compiled from the Original Returns of the Eighth Census, Under the Direction of the Secretary of the Interior.* Washington: Government Printing Office, 1865.

———. *Population of the United States in 1860; Compiled from the Original Returns of the Eighth Census, under the Direction of the Secretary of the Interior, By Joseph C. G. Kennedy, Superintendent of Census.* Washington: Government Printing Office, 1864.

———. *Preliminary Report on the Eighth Census, 1860. By Joseph C. G. Kennedy, Superintendent.* Washington: Government Printing Office, 1862.

U. S. Congress. House. 22nd Congress, 1st Session (1831–32). House Executive Document No. 308 (serial volumes 222 and 223). *Documents Relative to the Manufactures in the United States, Collected and Transmitted to the House of Representatives In compliance with a resolution of January 19, 1832, By the Secretary of the Treasury. In Two Volumes. Volume I. [II.] Printed by order of the House of Representatives.* 2 vols.; Washington: Duff Green, 1833. (Known as the "McLane Report.")

U. S. Congress. House. 24th Congress, 1st Session (1835–36). House Document No. 219 (serial volume 291). *Foreign Paupers. Report of a Committee and a Resolution of the House of Representatives of the State of Massachusetts, Upon the subject of the introduction into the United States of paupers from foreign countries.* Washington: Blair & Rives, 1836.

U. S. Congress. House. 26th Congress, 1st Session (1839–40). Document No. 38 (serial volume 364). *Sixth Census. Message from the President of the United States, Transmitting A Report from the Secretary of State, upon the subject of the law for taking the sixth census.* Washington: Blair & Rives, 1840.

U. S. Congress. House. 27th Congress, 2nd Session (1841–42). Document No. 23 (serial volume 401). *Sixth Census. Letter from the Secretary of State, Enclosing A Copy of the Sixth Census, as corrected and printed by the Department of State; also, a calculation for the Apportionment of Representatives, &c.* Washington: no publisher, 1841.

———. Document No. 91 (serial volume 402). *Statistics of the United States—Sixth Census. Letter from the Secretary of State, Transmitting A report upon the subject of the printing the statistics of the United States, taken under the acts relating to taking the sixth census.* Washington: no publisher, 1842.

———. Document No. 118 (serial volume 402). *Public Printing—Thomas Allen. Letter from Thomas Allen, In relation to the printing of the compendium of the sixth census.* Washington: no publisher, 1842.

———. Document No. 245 (serial volume 405). *Distribution of Returns of Sixth Census. Letter from the Secretary of State, Transmitting An Estimate of an appropriation which will be required for a distribution of the aggregate returns of the sixth census, &c.* Washington: no publisher, 1842.

———. Report No. 45 (serial volume 407). *Blair & Rives.* Washington: no publisher, 1842.

U. S. Congress. House. 28th Congress, 1st Session (1843–44). Document No. 245 (serial volume 443). *Sixth Census. Letter from the Secretary of State, In answer To a resolution of the House, inquiring whether errors have been discovered in the printed Sixth Census, as corrected at the Department of State in 1843.* Washington: Blair & Rives, 1845.

———. Report No. 301 (serial volume 445). *Bureau of Statistics and Commerce.* [*To accompany bill H. R. No. 212.*] Washington: Blair & Rives, 1844.

U. S. Congress. House. 28th Congress, 2nd Session (1844–45). Document No. 5 (serial volume 449). *Memorial of the American Statistical Association, Praying The adoption of measures for the correction of errors in the returns of the sixth census.* Washington: Gales & Seaton, 1845.

———. Document No. 116 (serial volume 465). *Errors in Sixth Census. Letter from the Secretary of State, Relative to Alleged errors of the Sixth Census.* Washington: Blair & Rives, 1845.

U. S. Congress. Senate. 21st Congress, 2nd Session (1830–31). Document No. 76 (serial volume 204). *Commerce and Navigation of the United States . . .* Washington: Duff Green, 1831.

U. S. Congress. Senate. 28th Congress, 2nd Session (1844–45). Document No. 146 (serial volume 457). *In Senate of the United States.* Washington: Gales & Seaton, 1845.

U. S. Congress. Senate. 32nd Congress, 1st Session (1851–52). Ex-

executive Document No. 112 (serial volume 622). *Communication from the Secretary of the Treasury, transmitting, in compliance with a resolution of the Senate of March 8, 1851, the Report of Israel D. Andrews, . . . , on the Trade and Commerce of the British North American Colonies, and upon the Trade of the Great Lakes and Rivers; . . . .* Washington: Robert Armstrong, 1853.

Wright, Carroll D., and William C. Hunt. *The History and Growth of the United States Census, prepared for the Senate Committee on the Census, by . . . .* Washington: Government Printing Office, 1900; reprinted, New York: Johnson Reprint Corp., 1966.

ARTICLES AND BOOKS

Adams, George (comp.). *Boston Directory for . . . .* (Titles vary.) Boston: George Adams, 1846–57; Adams, Sampson, & Co., 1858–61.

Albion, Robert G. *The Rise of New York Port [1815–1860]*. New York: Charles Scribner's Sons, 1939.

Arkin, Herbert, and Colton, Raymond R. (comps.). *Tables for Statisticians.* New York: Barnes & Noble, 1963.

Armstrong, W. A. "The Interpretation of the Census Enumerators' Books for Victorian Towns" in Harold J. Dyos (ed.). *The Study of Urban History*. London: Edward Arnold, Ltd., 1968. Pp. 67–85.

Benton, Josiah H. *Early Census Making in Massachusetts, 1643–1765, With a Reproduction of the Lost Census of 1765 (Recently Found) and Documents Relating Thereto; Now First Collected and Published by J. H. Benton, Jr.* Boston: C. E. Goodspeed, 1905.

The Berkshire Jubilee, Celebrated at Pittsfield, Mass. August 22 and 23, 1844. Albany: Weare, C. Little; Pittsfield: E. P. Little, 1845.

Bidwell, Percy W. "The Agricultural Revolution in [Southern] New England," *American Historical Review* 26 (July 1921), 683–702.

———. "Population Growth in Southern New England, 1810–1860," *American Statistical Association Publications* 15 (Dec. 1917), 813–39.

———. "Rural Economy in New England at the Beginning of the 19th Century," *Connecticut Academy of Arts Transactions* 20 (April 1916), 241–399.

Blake, John B. "The Early History of Vital Statistics in Massachusetts,"

Bulletin of the History of Medicine 29 (Jan.–Feb. 1955), 46–68.

Boeck, George A. "A Historical Note on the Uses of Census Returns," *Mid-America* 44 (Jan. 1962), 46–50.

Bonner, James C. "Profile of a Late Ante-Bellum Community," *American Historical Review* 49 (July 1944), 663–80.

Boston. Board of Trade. . . . *Annual Report of the Government, Presented to the Board at the Annual Meeting, on the . . . of January, 18 . . . .* Boston: Moore & Crosby, 1855–56; Geo. C. Rand & Avery, 1857–58; T. R. Marvin & Son, 1859; Wright & Potter, 1860; T. R. Marvin & Son, 1861; Alfred Mudge & Son, 1862.

Boston. Committee on the Expediency of Providing Better Tenements for the Poor. *Report of the Committee on the Expediency of Providing Better Tenements for the Poor.* Boston: Eastburn's Press, 1846.

Boston. Society for the Prevention of Pauperism. . . . *Annual Report of the Boston Society for the Prevention of Pauperism. October, 18 . . . .* 17th, 20th–25th, Boston: John Wilson & Son, 1852, 1855–60.

Bowen, Abel. *Bowen's Picture of Boston, or the Citizen's and Stranger's Guide to the Metropolis of Massachusetts, and its Environs. To Which is Affixed the Annals of Boston. Embellished With Engravings.* 3rd Edition; Boston: Otis, Broaders & Co., 1838.

Buckingham, Charles E. *Circumstances Affecting Individual and Public Health. A Lecture Delivered Before Suffolk Lodge, No. 8, Independent Order of Odd Fellows, On Tuesday Evening, April 11, 1848.* Boston: William Chadwick, 1848.

Bushée, Frederick A. "Ethnic Factors in the Population of Boston," *American Economic Association Publications* Third Series 4 (May 1903), 299–477.

———. "The Growth of the Population of Boston," *American Statistical Association Publications* 6 (June 1899), 239–74.

Chickering, Jesse. "Cities and Towns in the United States. Increase of the Thirty-Six Principal Cities and Towns," *Hunt's Merchants' Magazine* 10 (May 1844), 461–64.

———. *Immigration into the United States.* Boston: Charles C. Little & James Brown, 1848.

———. "The Progress of Wealth in Massachusetts, from 1790 to 1840," *Hunt's Merchants' Magazine* 16 (May 1847), 435–44.

———. *A Statistical View of the Population of Massachusetts, from 1765 to 1840.* Boston: Charles C. Little & James Brown, 1846.

[Clarke, Edward H.] "Sanitary Reform," *North American Review* 73 (July 1851), 117–35.

Cole, Donald B. *Immigrant City: Lawrence, Massachusetts, 1845–1921*. Chapel Hill: University of North Carolina Press, 1963.

Coleman, Peter J. "Restless Grant County [Wisconsin]: Americans on the Move," *Wisconsin Magazine of History* 46 (Autumn 1962), 16–20.

Conference on Research in Income and Wealth. *Output, Employment, and Productivity in the United States After 1800*. "Studies in Income and Wealth," vol. 30; New York: Columbia University Press for the National Bureau of Economic Research, 1966.

———. *Trends in the American Economy in the Nineteenth Century*. "Studies in Income and Wealth," vol. 24; Princeton: Princeton University Press for the National Bureau of Economic Research, 1960.

Coolidge, Austin J. (comp.). *Catalogue of the Lots in the Cemetery of Mount Auburn, Names of the Proprietors and Representatives of Deceased Proprietors; the Charter, By-Laws, Etc.* Boston: A. J. Mudge & Son, 1867.

Curti, Merle E., *et al. The Making of an American Community: A Case Study of Democracy in a Frontier County*. Stanford: Stanford University Press, 1959.

Curtis, Josiah. "On the System of Registration in the United States of America," [Royal] *Statistical Society of London Journal* 17 (March 1854), 43–44.

Darby, William, and Theodore Dwight, Jr. (comps.). *A New Gazetteer of the United States of America; Containing a Copious Description of the States, Territories, Counties, Parishes, Districts, Cities and Towns—Mountains, Lakes, Rivers and Canals—Commerce, Manufactures, Agriculture, and the Arts Generally, of the United States; . . . ; With the Population of 1830*. Hartford: Edward Hopkins, 1833.

Davenport, Bishop (comp.). *A History and New Gazetteer, or Geographical Dictionary, of North America and the West Indies, ... A New and Much Improved Edition*. New York: S. W. Benedict & Co., 1842.

Derby, Elias H. "Agriculture, and the Influence of Manufactures and Public Improvements on Agriculture," *Hunt's Merchants' Magazine* 17 (Dec. 1847), 547–59.

———. "Commercial Cities and Towns of the United States. Number XXII. City of Boston," *Hunt's Merchants' Magazine* 23 (Nov. 1850), 483–97.

Dollar, Charles M., and Richard J. Jensen. *Historian's Guide to Statistics Quantitative Analysis and Historical Research*. New York: Holt, Rinehart & Winston, 1971.

Dyos, Harold J. (ed.). *The Story of Urban History*. London: Edward Arnold, Ltd., 1968.

Evans, George H., Jr. "A Sketch of American Business Organization, 1832–1900," *Journal of Political Economy* 60 (Dec. 1952), 475–86.

——— and Walter C. Kanwisher, Jr. "Business Organization in Baltimore, 1859," *Journal of Political Economy* 62 (Feb. 1954), 63–67.

[Forbes, Abner] (comp.). *The Rich Men of Massachusetts: Containing A Statement of the Reputed Wealth of About Two Thousand Persons, with Brief Sketches of Nearly Fifteen Hundred Characters*. 2nd edition; Boston: Printed for Redding & Co., Hotchkiss & Co., Fetridge & Co., & W. V. Spencer, 1852.

——— and James W. Greene (comps.). *The Rich Men of Massachusetts: Containing A Statement of the Reputed Wealth of About Fifteen Hundred Persons, with Brief Sketches of More Than One Thousand Characters*. Boston: W. V. Spencer, 1851.

Gilchrist, David T. (ed.). *Growth of the Seaport Cities 1790–1825 Proceedings of a Conference Sponsored by the Eleutherian Mills-Hagley Foundation March 17–19, 1966*. Charlottesville: University Press of Virginia for the Eleutherian Mills-Hagley Foundation, 1967.

Gitelman, Howard M. "The Waltham System and the Coming of the Irish," *Labor History* 8 (Fall 1967), 227–53.

Glaab, Charles N., and A. Theodore Brown. *A History of Urban America*. New York: Macmillan, 1967.

Goldstein, Sidney. "City Directories As Sources of Migration Data," *American Journal of Sociology* 60 (Sept. 1954), 169–76.

———. "Migration: Dynamic of the American City," *American Quarterly* 6 (Winter 1954), 337–48.

———. *Patterns of Mobility 1910–1950 The Norristown Study A Method for Measuring Migration and Occupational Mobility in the Community*. Philadelphia: University of Pennsylvania Press, 1958.

———. "Repeated Migration as a Factor in High Mobility Rates," *American Sociological Review* 19 (Oct. 1954), 536–41.

Goodrich, Samuel G. (comp.). *A System of Universal Geography, Popular and Scientific, Comprising a Physical, Political, and*

Statistical Account of the World and its Various Divisions; . . . . 2 vols.; Boston: Carter, Hendee & Co., 1832.

Greenwald, William I. "The Ante-Bellum Population, 1830–1860," *Mid-America* 36 (July 1954), 176–89.

Gutman, Robert. "Birth and Death Registration in Massachusetts: I. The Colonial Background, 1639–1800; II. The Inauguration of a Modern System, 1800–1849; III. The System Achieves a Form, 1849–1869; IV. The System Attains its Basic Goals, 1870–1900," *Milbank Memorial Fund Quarterly* 36 (Jan. and Oct. 1958), 58–74, 373–402; 37 (July and Oct. 1959), 297–326, 386–417.

Hale, Edward E. *Letters on Irish Emigration. First Published in the Boston Daily Advertiser.* Boston: Phillips, Sampson & Co., 1852.

Handlin, Oscar. *Boston's Immigrants: A Study in Acculturation Revised and Enlarged Edition.* Cambridge: Harvard University Press, 1959.

——— and John Burchard (eds.). *The Historian and the City.* Cambridge: The M. I. T. Press, 1963.

Hansen, Marcus L. *The Atlantic Migration 1607–1860: A History of the Continuing Settlement of the United States.* Cambridge: Harvard University Press, 1940; reprinted, New York: Harper & Bros., 1961.

Hauser, Philip M., and Leo F. Schnore (eds.). *The Study of Urbanization.* New York: John Wiley & Sons, 1967.

Hayward, John (comp.). *A Gazetteer of Massachusetts, Containing Descriptions of All the Counties, Towns and Districts in the Commonwealth.* . . . Revised edition; Boston: John P. Jewett & Co., 1849.

——— (comp.). *A Gazetteer of the United States of America: Comprising a Concise General View of the United States . . . to Which Are Added Valuable Statistical Tables.* Philadelphia: James L. Gihon, 1854.

Hazen, Edward. *Popular Technology; or, Professions and Trades.* 2 vols.; New York: Harper & Bros., 1841.

Henretta, James A. "Economic Development and Social Structure in Colonial Boston," *William & Mary Quarterly,* Third Series 22 (Jan. 1965), 75–92.

Hine, L. A. "A General Statistical Society for the United States," *Hunt's Merchants' Magazine* 18 (April 1848), 397–402.

Hollingsworth, Thomas H. *Historical Demography.* Ithaca: Cornell University Press, 1969.

Huse, Charles P. *The Financial History of Boston, from May 1, 1822, to January 31, 1909*. "Harvard Economic Studies," Volume 15; Cambridge: Harvard University Press, 1916.

Hutchinson, Ruth G., Arthur R. Hutchinson, and Mabel Newcomer. "A Study in Business Mortality: Length of Life of Business Enterprises in Poughkeepsie, New York, 1843–1936," *American Economic Review* 28 (Sept. 1938), 497–514.

Jarvis, Edward. [Review of Massachusetts Registration Reports, 1850, 1841–49; New York Registration Reports, 1847, 1848; and a Memorial to the Louisiana Legislature], *American Journal of Medical Sciences* 24 (July 1852), 147–64.

———. [Review of Massachusetts Registration Reports, 1851, 1852; Connecticut Registration Reports, 1848/49–1850/51; New Jersey Registration Reports, 1851–53; Kentucky Registration Report, 1852], *American Journal of Medical Sciences* 29 (April 1855), 407–30.

Johnson, Arthur M., and Barry E. Supple. *Boston Capitalists and Western Railroads: A Study in the Nineteenth-Century Railroad Investment Process*. Cambridge: Harvard University Press, 1967.

Kennedy, Charles J. "Commuter Services in the Boston Area, 1835–1860," *Business History Review* 36 (Summer 1962), 153–70.

Kennedy, Joseph C. G. *Progress of Statistics; Read Before the American Geographical & Statistical Society, at the Annual Meeting in New York, Dec. 1, 1859*. New York: J. O. Trow, 1861. Appeared also as *American Geographical Society Journal* 2 (July 1860), 92–120.

———. *Review of the Report of the Senate Committee on the Returns of the Seventh Census*. Washington: Gideon & Co., 1852.

Kett, Joseph F. "Growing Up in Rural New England, 1800–1840," in Tamara K. Hareven (ed.). *Anonymous Americans: Explorations in Nineteenth-Century Social History*. Englewood Cliffs, N. J.: Prentice-Hall, 1971. Pp. 1–16.

King, Moses (comp.). *King's Hand-Book of Boston Profusely Illustrated*. Cambridge: Moses King, 1879.

Kirkland, Edward C. *Men, Cities and Transportation: A Study in New England History 1820–1900*. 2 vols.; Cambridge: Harvard University Press, 1948.

Lane, Roger. *Policing the City Boston 1822–1885*. Cambridge: Harvard University Press, 1967.

Lathrop, Barnes F. "History from the Census Returns," *Southwestern Historical Quarterly* 51 (April 1948), 293–312.

Lebergott, Stanley. *Manpower in Economic Growth: The American Record since 1800*. New York: McGraw-Hill, 1964.

Lee, Everett S. "A Theory of Migration," *Demography* 3 (No. 1, 1966), 47–57.

——— and Anne S. Lee, "Internal Migration Statistics for the United States," *Journal of the American Statistical Association* 55 (Dec. 1960), 664–97.

Lord, Robert H., John E. Sexton, and Edward T. Harrington. *History of the Archdiocese of Boston In the Various Stages of Its Development 1604 to 1943*. 3 vols.; Boston: The Pilot Publishing Co., 1945.

McKelvey, Blake F. *Rochester, The Flower City 1855–1890*. Cambridge: Harvard University Press, 1949.

Malin, James C. *The Grassland of North America Prolegomena to its History With Addenda and Postscript*. Gloucester: Peter Smith, 1967.

———. "The Turnover of Farm Population in Kansas," *The Kansas Historical Quarterly* 4 (Nov. 1935), 339–72.

Midgley, R. L. (comp.). *Boston Sights; Or, Hand-Book for Visitors*. Boston: A. Williams & Co., 1865.

Montgomery, David. "The Working Classes of the Pre-Industrial American City, 1780–1830," *Labor History* 9 (Winter 1968), 3–22.

Morison, Samuel E. *The Maritime History of Massachusetts 1783–1860*. 2nd edition; Boston: Houghton Mifflin Sentry Editions, 1961.

Moroney, M. J. *Facts from Figures*. Baltimore: Penguin Books, 1965.

North, Douglas C. *The Economic Growth of the United States 1790–1860*. Englewood Cliffs, N. J.: Prentice-Hall, 1961.

———. *Growth and Welfare in the American Past: A New Economic History*. Englewood Cliffs, N. J.: Prentice-Hall, 1966.

"Our First Men:" A Calendar of Wealth, Fashion and Gentility; Containing a List of Those Persons Taxed in the City of Boston Credibly Reported to be Worth One Hundred Thousand Dollars, with Biographical Notices of the Principal Persons. Boston: All the Booksellers, 1846.

Owsley, Frank L. *Plain Folk of the Old South*. Baton Rouge: Louisiana State University Press, 1949; reprinted, Chicago: Quadrangle Books, 1965.

Pred, Allan R. *The Spatial Dynamics of U. S. Urban-Industrial Growth, 1800–1914: Interpretive and Theoretical Essays*. Cambridge: The M. I. T. Press, 1966.

Rand Corporation (comp.). *A Million Random Digits with 100,000 Normal Deviates*. Glencoe, Ill.: The Free Press, 1955.

Ravenstein, E. G. "The Laws of Migration," [Royal] *Statistical Society of London Journal* 48 (June 1885), 167–227 (and discussion, 228–35).

———. "The Laws of Migration," [Royal] *Statistical Society of London Journal* 52 (June 1889), 241–301.

Redford, Arthur. *Labour Migration in England 1800–1850.* 2nd edition revised; Manchester: Manchester University Press, 1964.

Salsbury, Stephen. *The State, the Investor, and the Railroad: The Boston & Albany, 1825–1867.* Cambridge: Harvard University Press, 1967.

Savage, Edward H. (comp.). *Boston Events. A Brief Mention and the Date of More than 5,000 Events that Transpired in Boston From 1630 to 1880, Covering a Period of 250 Years, Together with other Occurrences of Interest, arranged in Alphabetical Order.* Boston: Tolman & White, 1884.

Schlesinger, Arthur M., Sr. *The Rise of the City 1878–1898.* New York: Macmillan, 1933.

Schnore, Leo F. "Problems in the Quantitative Study of Urban History" in Harold J. Dyos (ed.). *The Study of Urban History.* London: Edward Arnold, Ltd., 1968. Pp. 189–208.

Seaman, Ezra C. *Essays on the Progress of Nations, in Civilization, Productive Industry, Wealth and Population. Illustrated by Statistics of Mining, Agriculture, Manufactures, Commerce, Coin, Banking, Internal Improvements, Emigration and Population.* New York: Charles Scribner, 1852; reprinted, New York: Johnson Reprint Corp., 1967.

Shurtleff, Nathaniel B. *A Topographical and Historical Description of Boston.* Boston: A. Williams & Co., 1871.

Smelser, Marshall, and William Davisson. "The Historian and the Computer: A Simple Introduction to Complex Computation," *Essex Institute Historical Collections* 104 (April 1968), 109–26.

Smith, Walter Buckingham, and Arthur Harrison Cole. *Fluctuations in American Business 1790–1860.* Cambridge: Harvard University Press, 1935.

Snow, Caleb H. *A Geography of Boston, County of Suffolk and The Adjacent Towns. With Historical Notes. By C. H. Snow, M. D. Author of the History of Boston. With Maps and Plates. For the Younger Class of Readers.* Boston: Carter & Hendee, 1830.

Sons of New Hampshire. *Festival of the Sons of New Hampshire: With the Speeches of Messrs. Webster, Woodbury, Wilder, Bigelow, Parker, Dearborn, Hubbard, Goodrich, Hale, Plummer, Wilson, Chamberlain, and Others, Together with the Names of Those*

Present, and Letters from Distinguished Individuals. Celebrated in Boston, November 7, 1849. Phonographic Report by Dr. James W. Stone, President of the Boston Reporting Association. Boston: James French, 1850.

———. *Second Festival of the Sons of New Hampshire, Celebrated in Boston, November 2, 1853; Including Also an Account of the Proceedings in Boston on the Day of the Funeral at Marshfield, and the Subsequent Obsequies Commemorative of the Death of Daniel Webster, Their Late President. Phonographic Report by Alexander C. Felton.* Boston: James French & Co., 1854.

Spear, Dorothea N. (comp.). *Bibliography of American* [City] *Directories Through 1860.* Worcester: American Antiquarian Society, 1961.

Stilwell, Lewis D. *Migration from Vermont.* Montpelier: Vermont Historical Society, 1948. Appeared also as *Vermont Historical Society Proceedings* 5 (June 1937), 63–246.

Stimpson, Charles (comp.). *The Boston Directory.* Boston: Charles Stimpson, Jr., 1830.

———. (comp.). *Stimpson's Boston Directory.* Boston: Charles Stimpson, Jr., 1831–46.

Taylor, George Rogers. "American Urban Growth Preceding the Railway Age," *Journal of Economic History* 27 (Sept. 1967), 309–39.

———. "The Beginnings of Mass Transportation in Urban America: Part I [II]," *Smithsonian Journal of History* 1 (Summer and Autumn 1966), 35–50 and 31–54.

———. *The Transportation Revolution 1815–1860.* "The Economic History of the United States," volume 4; New York: Rinehart & Co., 1951.

Texas. University. Bureau of Research in the Social Sciences. *The Use of City Directories in the Study of Urban Populations: A Methodological Note.* "University of Texas Publication" No. 4202; Austin: University of Texas, 1942.

Thernstrom, Stephan A. *Poverty and Progress Social Mobility in a Nineteenth Century City.* Cambridge: Harvard University Press, 1964.

———. "Urbanization, Migration, and Social Mobility in Late Nineteenth-Century America" in Barton J. Bernstein (ed.). *Towards a New Past: Dissenting Essays in American History.* New York: Pantheon Books, 1968. Pp. 158–75.

——— and Peter R. Knights. "Men in Motion: Some Data and Speculations about Urban Population Mobility in Nineteenth-Century America," *Journal of Interdisciplinary History* 1 (Autumn 1970), 7–35, and in Tamara K. Hareven (ed.). *Anonymous Americans: Explorations in Nineteenth-Century Social History*. Englewood Cliffs, N. J.: Prentice-Hall, 1971. Pp. 17–47.

——— and Sennett, Richard (eds.). *Nineteenth-Century Cities: Essays in the New Urban History*. New Haven: Yale University Press, 1969.

Tucker, George. "A General Statistical Society for the United States," *Hunt's Merchants' Magazine* 17 (Dec. 1847), 571–77.

———. "The Next Census of the United States," *Hunt's Merchants' Magazine* 19 (Nov. 1848), 523–27.

———. *Progress of the United States in Population and Wealth in Fifty Years, as Exhibited by the Decennial Census from 1790–1840 . . . With an Appendix, Containing an Abstract of the Census of 1850*. New York: Press of Hunt's Merchants' Magazine, 1855; reprinted, New York: Augustus M. Kelley, Publisher, 1964.

Walsh, Margaret. "The Census as an Accurate Source of Information: The Value of Mid-Nineteenth Century Manufacturing Returns," *Historical Methods Newsletter* 3 (Sept. 1970), 3–13.

———. "The Value of Mid-Nineteenth Century Manufacturing Returns: The Printed Census and the Manuscript Census Compilations Compared," *Historical Methods Newsletter* 4 (March 1971), 43–51.

Ward, David. *Cities and Immigrants: A Geography of Change in Nineteenth-Century America*. New York: Oxford University Press, 1971.

———. "The Emergence of Central Immigrant Ghettoes in American Cities: 1840–1920," *Annals of the Association of American Geographers* 58 (June 1968), 343–59.

———. "The Industrial Revolution and the Emergence of Boston's Central Business District," *Economic Geography* 42 (April 1966), 152–71.

Ware, Norman J. *The Industrial Worker 1840–1860: The Reaction of American Industrial Society to the Advance of the Industrial Revolution*. Boston: Houghton Mifflin Co., 1924; reprinted, Chicago: Quadrangle Books, 1964.

Warner, Sam B., Jr. "If All the World Were Philadelphia: A Scaffolding for Urban History, 1774–1930," *American Historical Review* 74 (October 1968), 26–43.

———. *The Private City Philadelphia in Three Periods of Its Growth*. Philadelphia: University of Pennsylvania Press, 1968.

———. *Streetcar Suburbs: The Process of Growth in Boston, 1870–1900*. Cambridge: Harvard University Press, 1962.

Weber, Adna F. *The Growth of Cities in the Nineteenth Century: A Study in Statistics*. "Columbia University Studies in History, Economics and Public Law" No. 11; New York: The Macmillan Co., 1899; reprinted, Ithaca: Cornell University Press, 1963.

Webster, Noah. *An American Dictionary of the English Language* . . . . Springfield, Mass.: George & Charles Merriam, 1852.

Whelpton, Pascal K. "Occupational Groups in the United States, 1820–1920," *Journal of the American Statistical Association* 21 (Sept. 1926), 335–43.

Whitehill, Walter M. *Boston: A Topographical History*. Cambridge: Harvard University Press, 1959.

Williamson, Jeffrey G. "Antebellum Urbanization in the American Northeast," *Journal of Economic History* 25 (Dec. 1965), 592–608.

——— and Swanson, Joseph A. "The Growth of Cities in the American Northeast, 1820–1870," *Explorations in Entrepreneurial History*, Second Series 4 (No. 1, Supplement, 1966), 1–101.

Wilson, Harold F. *The Hill Country of Northern New England Its Social and Economic History 1790–1930*. New York: Columbia University Press, 1936; reprinted, New York: AMS Press, Inc., 1967.

[Wilson, Thomas L. V.] *The Aristocracy of Boston: Who They Are, and What They Were: Being A History of the Business and Business Men of Boston, for the Last Forty Years. By One Who Knows Them*. Boston: The Author, 1848.

Winsor, Justin (ed.). *The Memorial History of Boston, Including Suffolk County, Massachusetts, 1630–1880*. 4 vols.; Boston: Ticknor & Co., 1880–81.

Worthman, Paul B. "Working Class Mobility in Birmingham, Alabama, 1880–1914," in Tamara K. Hareven (ed.). *Anonymous Americans: Explorations in Nineteenth-Century Social History*. Englewood Cliffs, N. J.: Prentice-Hall, 1971. Pp. 172–213.

The Plain People of Boston: An Afterword

The history of plain and proper Bostonians in the ante-bellum years is inseparable from the economic and social changes sweeping the New England region. During and after the War of 1812 business initiatives and capital resources originating in the old commercial center on Massachusetts Bay launched the larger hinterland upon a course of industrialization as rapid and thoroughgoing in its effect as that which had occurred in parts of the British Isles half a century before. As in Britain, moreover, the industrial revolution in North America had its first notable impact on the production of textiles. It was the singular achievement of Yankee merchants to combine the labor power of a fast-growing rural population with their region's abundant water power in the manufacture of cheap cotton cloth out of raw fiber imported from the distant Southern states. Boston was the hub of the industrial revolution in New England.

The inauguration of the revolution is symbolized in the new "integrated" mills built a few miles up the Charles River at Waltham by the Boston Manufacturing Company between 1813 and 1818. The Boston group opened their mill at the confluence of the Merrimack and Concord Rivers (later called Lowell) in 1823 and built another at Chicopee on the Connecticut River in the same year. The rapid growth in the output of cotton cloth over the two decades after 1813 (as well as in the preceding Embargo and War years) indicates, however, that merchants and mechanics elsewhere in New England were no less alive to the expansive possibilities of industrial organization than the great capitalists from the hub. The natural endowments of the region were limited, and the basis of prewar prosperity in the "neutral" trade had disappeared once Europe had returned to peace in 1815.

The growing population of the seaboard states provided only part of the market for New England's industrial goods. A further impetus was received from the spread of settlement into the trans-Applachian West where new areas of agricultural colonization could not at once develop a specialized manufacturing base of their own and meanwhile lacked a strong base of rural industry such as had characterized the thickly settled New England states for more than a century before the industrial revolution. Improvements in steam navigation on Western rivers, construction of overland routes from the seaboard, and the growth of river and canal systems across New York enlarged the territorial extent of, and lessened the cost of access to, the potential markets of the interior.

The demand for New England's cotton goods far exceeded the region's initial capacities. Physical output of cotton cloth rose tenfold between 1818 and 1826 and then experienced a more gradual tenfold increase again over the years to 1860. These demands could not have been realized as rapidly as they were in the early years without the technical and organizational innovations represented by the improved power loom and three or four other mechanical novelties which facilitated the integration of power spinning and weaving in single establishments "on the Waltham Plan." By the mid-1820's virtually all of the region's cloth woven from native yarns was factory produced at from a half to a quarter the cost per yard of material finished under the domestic regime. While the high prices and profit margins of the early 1820's had fallen off by the 1830's, the returns to capital invested in textiles sufficed to assure a gradual increase in the region's capacity—without much further benefit from technical innovation—down through the ante-bellum years.

By 1840 nearly 40 per cent of the New England work force was specialized away from agricultural production. Since the war, in fact, the populations of Massachusetts, Rhode Island, and Connecticut had become even more dependent on manufacturing employment than their contemporaries in New York or Pennsylvania where large tracts had become available for farming in the west. Non-agricultural income per worker in New England, excluding income from commerce, was more than a third above the national level in 1840 and exceeded the levels obtaining in the larger and more richly endowed regions centering on New York City, Philadelphia, and New Orleans. But just as Boston and its merchant entrepreneurs were not the sole pioneers of industrialism in New England, so cotton cloth was not the region's only industrial product. In 1840, to be sure, the various branches of the cotton industry contributed almost two-thirds of the "value added" by New England factory production, but by that date the impact of industrialization had become cumulative and pervasive. Numerous other activities were experiencing industrial reorganization, many directly influenced by the example of cotton goods. "In 1840," wrote Percy Bidwell, "it would have been difficult to find 50 out of 479 townships in Southern New England which did not have at least one manufacturing village clustered around a cotton or a woolen mill, an iron furnace, a chair factory or a carriage shop, or some other representative . . . of manufactures which had grown up in haphazard fashion in every part of the three states." *

By the close of the ante-bellum period New England enjoyed the highest average level of personal incomes in the nation, having surpassed both the Middle Atlantic and South Western regions after 1840. In 1860, moreover, the population of New England was almost 37 per cent urbanized, while the primary manufacturing states of Rhode Island and Massachusetts already had half their populations concentrated in "cities" of 2500 or more residents before mid-century. The flood of the foreign-born which had begun to swell the region's population around 1850 also concentrated in

* "The Agricultural Revolution in New England," *American Historical Review*, Vol. XXVI (1921), page 686.

the cities or moved on rapidly with migrants of native birth to other parts of the Union. Finally, during the decade of the Civil War, the rural populations of both the manufacturing states and the region as a whole entered on an absolute decline. Thereafter, the continued increase of Boston's plain people, as well as the urban transformation of the region, were largely dependent on the demographic contributions of immigrants and their children.

Meanwhile Boston had grown up with the region and the nation. Her capitalists invested in Western lands, mineral and forest resources, canals and railroads, as well as in the manufacturing and transportation revolutions nearer home. Railway connections were opened in the mid-1830's with Worcester, Lowell, and Providence, with Albany in 1841, with Fitchburg in 1845, and with the Great Lakes and Canada by 1851. In 1840 Boston was selected as the trans-Atlantic terminus of the Cunard steamship line. Although the commerce of the port slackened in the late 1850's, it continued to be the nation's second largest port. Boston remained the nation's largest wholesale market for wool and fish, and for almost all other commodities it was the most important regional emporium. Boston likewise dominated the region's finances throughout the ante-bellum period and, while challenged increasingly by the colossus on the Hudson, it was still much the largest redemption center for New England under the National Bank Act of 1864. Providence, Rhode Island, the region's second city since the 1820's when it overtook Salem in size, had barely 50,000 residents in 1860 and could not aspire to redemption status. But Boston was not only New England's historic "central place" and the principal headquarters for its textile industry, it was also a manufacturing city in its own right. There was work to be had in printing and publishing trades, in sugar refining, malt liquors, and confectionery, in the manufacture of mens' and womens' clothing, boots and shoes, in shipbuilding and related trades. Boston was famous for its musical instruments, including Chickering pianos and Mason and Hamlin reed organs; it was the home of the Singer sewing machine, and the Waltham watch was first made in nearby Roxbury. Compared with most New England cities Boston had a small share of its work force—less than a quarter in 1860—engaged in manufactures; but Yankee cities were mostly small places, little more than overgrown mill towns. Boston apart, only Providence, New Haven, and Lowell, all considerable manufacturing centers, had more than 30,000 inhabitants.

For all the social and economic transformation of New England in the ante-bellum era, the growth of Boston was not rapid. It ranked eighth among the ten major cities having the largest population increase in the years 1830–60 (Table II-3). However, unlike Baltimore in the decades before 1830 or New Orleans, Philadelphia, Chicago, or St. Louis in the years to 1860, Boston annexed little territory and virtually no population. Only New York among major cities gained less from political annexations than Boston over the first two-thirds of the century. Before its large annexations in 1868 and 1874 Boston had mostly enlarged its land surface by huge public works; the filling-in of tidal flats began as early as 1804, more was accomplished in the 1830's, and the spectacular reclamation of the Back Bay extended over three decades after 1856. Bostonians claimed that, as late as 1875, they had spent more on reducing, leveling, and reclaiming land surfaces, together with straightening and widening main thoroughfares, than had been spent for similar purposes by all the other chief cities combined.

If the comparison is made, not of city populations alone but of the larger "metropolitan areas" as well, then Boston appears to have regained third place behind greater New York and Philadelphia during the 1830's and to have held on to that rank until displaced by Chicago in 1880. In 1860, for example, when the population of Boston proper was under 178,000, that of the city and adjacent towns already exceeded 228,000. Notwithstanding the remarkable "churning" of the plain people in and out of the city, their *net* concentration in and around the hub continued long after 1860. Noted by Shattuck and Chickering as early as the 1830's and '40's, the process had concentrated 40 per cent of Massachusetts' population within a ten-mile radius of the state house by 1900, at which time greater Boston already exceeded 900,000.

The Plain People of Boston reveals the extent to which even the modest growth of the city before 1860 was dependent on migration. The contribution of native Bostonians to Knights's sample population peaks in 1840 at 17.3 per cent and declines to 10.7 per cent in 1860 (Table III-3). The balance, therefore, is always made up of people born outside the city who happen to be resident heads of household at the time of a census. Before the late 1840's the majority of migrants appear to have been native-born and mostly of rural origin. As late as 1850 the proportion of sample Bostonians born elsewhere in Massachusetts or New England is 40 per cent with a mere 2 per cent at most born elsewhere in the Union. But from the late 1840's the influx of foreigners, mostly Irish rural folk, is registered in the rising share of foreign-born in the sample, reaching 55 per cent in 1860, although the general population census credits the foreign-born with only 36 per cent of the city's residents in that year. In Table III-1 Knights shows clearly how the conventional distinction between native- and foreign-born understates the full alien contribution to the city's growth. In 1855, for example, 61 per cent of the population is given as native-born, but only 47 per cent turns out to be native-born of native parentage. These proportions tell nothing directly concerning relative contributions of natural increase and migration to the city's net growth in the years 1830–60. Since we can rule out annexation in the ante-be lum years, however, Knights's data do not seem inconsistent with a post-bellum estimate, based on the *49th Registration Report*, 1890, that natural increase contributed roughly 20 per cent of Boston's incremental growth between 1865 and 1890 as against 50 per cent from net migration with the balance from annexation.

All Knights's findings confirm the "locomotive habits" of the people. He is right to insist that the periodic census reveals no more than the *net* of all interim moves: in- and out-migration, births and deaths. While the net of social and natural movements generally suffices for most structural analyses of urbanization, it certainly obscures much that is vital in the history of cities and of urban society. Perhaps his most striking point is that every other year or so, up to one-half the members of Boston's population may "disappear" from the city and be replaced by in-migrants and new births. This gives a population turnover in the course of a decade that amounts to several times the city's initial population. Persistence rates for sample heads of households—not a particularly footloose class of men and women—range between 36 and 45 per cent in the ante-bellum decades (Table IV-10). While Boston's position as a port of entry and hub of a transport network, as well as the nature of the sources, may tend to heighten the aggregate motion somewhat, the temporary and transient involvement of so large a fraction of the adult population in a city's life and livelihood must become an important datum for future studies in U.S. urban history. Of scarcely lesser significance are the volume and frequency of circulatory moves within the city's boundaries and the continuous redistribution between central and peripheral areas of different nativity groups in the population (Tables IV-13, 14, and 15). In all of these currents the foreign-born are as mobile as the natives, much more so around the mid-century when their physical distribution throughout the city approximates closely that of the total population (Table IV-1).

Residential movements, of course, are by no means equivalent to social moves. The gradual decentralization of residence is rising in the 1830's and '40's, is arrested under the impact of massive immigration at mid-century, and then reasserts itself again before 1860. Part of this drift as George Adams, the compiler of city directories, remarked was a consequence of the encroachment of stores and warehouses on some of the inner residential districts, while the outward shift of manufacturing establishments and the notable increase in their scale of operations in the 1850's is further evidence of competition for inner space (Table VII-2). The need for unskilled casual labor in the port and commercial districts, however, tends to hold people near the center and leads to "doubling up" and general overcrowding as the poorer element accommodates the pressures on its habitat. But even in an age remarkable for the "multiplied conveniences of traveling," some of the wealthiest citizens (in terms of property tax assessments) maintain their residence close to the heart of the old city. In general it is the lower-middle and middling strata (in tax terms) who seek more peripheral residences in the ante-bellum years. The people most likely to quit the city altogether after 1840 are usually unskilled persons with little or no taxable property, while the exodus of some members of the proprietary and managerial classes does not generally occur before the 1850's (Tables VI-2, 3). Naturally enough it was at this point that the Council's Committee on Public Lands begins the familiar complaint about the loss of city population and tax revenues. (In Table VI-7, incidentally, Knights reports some preliminary findings concerning locations of those out-migrants whom he has traced to new residences up to 50 miles and more outside the city!)

Although Knights does employ occupational titles to indicate broad socioeconomic status differences, he is properly diffident in applying sociological notions and measures of "social mobility." The relation between job rubrics and class is at best an approximation of reality and never more so than during a period of industrial revolution when old nomenclatures take on new meanings and almost all social and economic relationships are subjected to great strain. The taxable wealth and social status of persons grouped by occupational title might vary considerably with age and stage of the life cycle. Certain classes of skilled and unskilled workers, as well as petty proprietors, in the sample do appear to be characteristically younger men. It is significant that the socioeconomic composition of four property assessment groups varies closely with age at each of four enumerations between 1830 and 1860: the wealthier the assessment group, the higher the socioeconomic status and median age of its membership (Table V-3). No precise measurement of social mobility would be possible unless the age structure of each socioeconomic group were taken into account. The use of cohort analysis would shed further light of "success" in ante-bellum Boston, but in several instances the sample number in a group becomes too small for any definite conclusion to be reached for periods of more than one decade.

There is little direct evidence on differential chances of "success" between native- and foreign-born residents. Most of the foreign-born are recent arrivals, however, and their low socioeconomic status would be as much the result of their lack of skills or outright illiteracy as of their exploitation by Yankee employers. There is a marked increase in size of the "unskilled and menial service" group around mid-century, but its size is already shrinking again before 1860. But of one recognizable "group" among the plain people, the Negro, there is little doubt of their inferior status or exploitation. Unlike the large and physically mobile immigrant population, the small Negro population is always confined to a few restricted neighborhoods (Table II-11). It is dependent for the most part on menial as well as casual employment, and this again suffices to inhibit its mobility. The predicament of the blacks was well stated by Jesse Chickering: while their "legal rights are the same as those of the whites, their condition is one of degredation and dependence." Even though articulate opinion seems to have changed from hostility to general sympathy for the abolitionist cause between the 1830's and the '50's, Boston's 2,000-odd Negroes remained largely invisible men and women.

Meanwhile, in the eyes of proper Bostonians their city remained the cultural hub of the universe. The tradition of the old *North American Review* had been strengthened in 1857 with the publication of the *Atlantic Monthly*. The Boston Museum was the scene of successful theatrical productions from the early 1840's, and the Boston Theater commenced its performances in 1854; the music of the Handel and Haydn Society was augmented in the late '30's by the Harvard Musical Association. The revival of the Public Library after 1848, the enlargement of the state house in the mid-50's, and the glory of the Public Garden laid out in 1859 on some 24 acres of newly filled land testify, along with the endowment of private philanthropies and learned societies, to the quality of Boston's civic spirit in the early industrial era. Educational opportunities were similarly enhanced by the founding of the Lowell Institute in 1839, the Massachusetts College of Pharmacy in 1852, and the opening of Boston College under the Society of Jesus in 1860. The Massachusetts Institute of Technology received a charter in 1861 and opened its doors a few years later to men and women intent on scientific and technical careers. It is ironic perhaps, in view of Chickering's description of conditions among the city's Negro residents, to recall that this Boston was also the home of Garrison's *Liberator*, of William Ellery Channing and of Wendell Phillips. Yet the city's association with the great anti-slavery movement also reminds us that, in Aristotle's words, a true city is always—in aspiration at least—"a common life for a noble end." Ante-bellum Boston was never a *polis,* but it was much more than the economic and social movements of its plain people.

ERIC E. LAMPARD

Index

(The Index includes the Introduction, Chapters I–VII, Appendices A–E, and the Notes, but not the Tables. A few persons, appearing in the above sections, also were indexed where they appeared in the Acknowledgments. Life dates appear for most nineteenth-century individuals.)